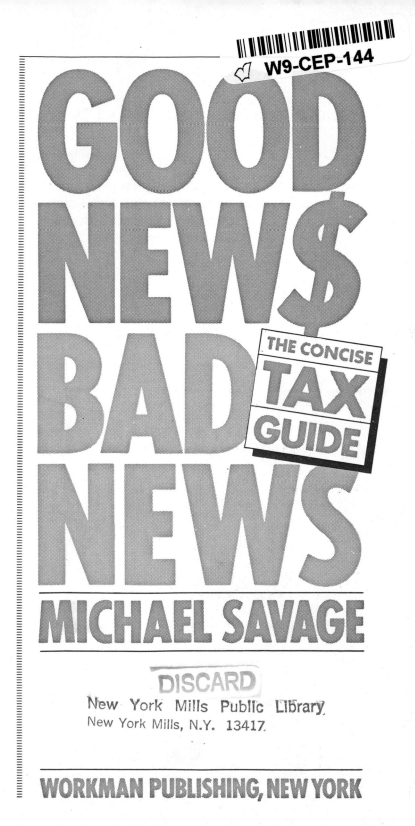

GOOD NEW$ BAD NEWS

THE CONCISE TAX GUIDE

MICHAEL SAVAGE

WORKMAN PUBLISHING, NEW YORK

ACKNOWLEDGEMENTS

The author wishes to thank Alan J. Strauss, CPA, Tax Partner at the Edward Isaacs and Co., New York, and attorney Murray Frank for their assistance in the technical editing of the book, and Arlene Dickens and Veneta Saunders for their assistance in its production.

Copyright © 1986 by Michael Savage

Library of Congress Cataloging-in-Publication Data
Savage, Michael, 1946-
Good news, bad news.
Includes index.
1. Income tax—Law and legislation—United States.
I. Title.
KF6369.S28   1986   343.7305'2   86-28160
ISBN 0-89480-294-1 (pbk.)   347.30352

Cover design: Charles Kreloff
Book design: Heather Gilchrist
Book illustration: Anders Wenngren

Anyone interested in subscribing to *Taxes Interpreted* ($197.00 for 26 bi-weekly issues) should write to Mr. Savage at 150 E. 58 St., 26th floor, N.Y., N.Y. 10155. (After January 31, 1987 write to 575 Lexington Avenue, 27th floor, N.Y., N.Y. 10022.)

Workman Publishing Company, Inc.
1 West 39th Street
New York, NY 10018

Manufactured in the United States of America
First printing November 1986

10 9 8 7 6 5 4 3 2 1

To Mariana

CONTENTS

INTRODUCTION

The 1986 Tax Reform Act is nearly 1,000 pages long. It is the most comprehensive revision of the federal income tax laws since World War II, and it affects virtually everybody who pays taxes.

How does it affect you? And how are you supposed to find out? Massive changes in an already complicated tax system may strike you as more than you can deal with. But tax reform is not as overwhelming as it seems. While the Act is nearly 1,000 pages long, less than 200 of those pages have any affect at all on the great majority of people. Much of the bill concerns only multinational corporations, banks, corporate pension plan administrators, insurance companies, and state and local government agencies that issue revenue bonds. There's no need for the typical American taxpayer, or even the typical American entrepreneur, to immerse himself in any of that.

More important, the new law does not change the structure of the tax code. When you do your income tax return you will still add up all your income, reduce it by your business deductions, reduce it further by your itemized deductions or by the standard deduction, claim your exemptions, and figure out your tax. Differences will occur only within this overall structure: more items of income will count as income; some expenses will no longer be deductible; others will have to pass more rigorous tests before they become deductible. As you tackle your tax return, you will recognize the subject matter of most of the rules—but you will realize that the rules themselves have changed.

The fact that the structure of the tax code has

remained the same does not mean that tax reform will not have an impact on you. For most of us it will have an enormous impact. And the questions that people want answers to are: "Do all these changes help me or hurt me? Do I pay more or less tax? Are the tax laws simpler, or do I still need professional help every year? Are my present investments affected? What do I do now?"

We will try to answer these questions, and more. Getting on top of tax reform is not impossible. It just looks impossible. We will take it one step at a time. For each change that is likely to affect you, we will examine what the law was before tax reform, how the 1986 tax law alters it, and what the change means to you. We will cover a great deal of material, but we will not cover every change in the tax law because that would be a rewrite of the tax reform act, and not much help. Only your tax advisor can tell you of every tax reform change that you personally need to know, but we will certainly show you how to deal with most of them.

Whether you pay more or less tax under tax reform will depend on you—on who you are, what you earn, and on how you choose to react to tax reform. With proper planning, you will still be able to hold your taxes to a minimum under the new law. The important thing is to know what is going on here. Once you know what is going on, what to do about it will be apparent.

CHAPTER ONE

REPEAL OF THE TAX BRACKETS

The 1986 Tax Reform Act repeals most of the "tax brackets" in the income tax laws—and the repeal of the tax brackets is no doubt the most significant feature of the new law. Before tax reform, the U.S. income tax system was a "progressive" tax system. Under this progressive system, as your income climbed, it got taxed at higher rates. As you added to your taxable income, the government took a greater part of the *addition*. The social justification of a progressive tax system is that people should pay tax at whatever rates they can afford—therefore, people who earn more money pay taxes at higher rates.

The U.S. tax system was not just a little progressive. It was highly progressive—the rates of tax rose rapidly with relatively small increases in income. In order to have a highly progressive tax system, you needed lots of tax brackets. And that was what we had. The progressive tax rates on taxable income in 1985 for married couples are shown in the accompanying box.

TAX RATES FOR MARRIED COUPLES IN 1985

TAXABLE INCOME	TAX RATE	TAXABLE INCOME	TAX RATE
$ 0–$ 3,540	0%	$ 31,120–$ 36,630	28%
3,540– 5,720	11%	36,630– 47,670	33%
5,720– 7,910	12%	47,670– 62,450	38%
7,910– 12,390	14%	62,450– 89,090	42%
12,390– 16,650	16%	89,090– 113,860	45%
16,650– 21,020	18%	113,860– 169,020	49%
21,020– 25,600	22%	over $169,020	50%
25,600– 31,120	25%		

The 14 tax brackets applied only to married couples who filed joint returns. But there were 14 different brackets for single people, and 14 still different brackets for heads of households. Married people who filed separate returns had 14 brackets of their own.

In the tax reform bill, Congress decided that having all these tax brackets was too complicated. Congress also recognized that people spent a great deal of time and effort looking for scores of deductions that would bring their taxable income down into a lower bracket. The solution, Congress thought, was to repeal many of the deductions—or at least make it more difficult to use them—and eliminate most of the tax brackets and set new, lower brackets. Later on, we will look at how Congress attacked all those deductions. As for the tax brackets, Congress repealed 12 of them, leaving only a 15% bracket and a 28% bracket.

Married couples

Under the new tax reform law, starting in 1988 (we'll talk about 1987 momentarily), the two tax rates for married people filing a joint return are: 15% on taxable income from $0 to $29,750; and 28% on taxable income over $29,750. Period. A surviving spouse—a recent widow or widower with children living at home—pays tax at the same rates. Married taxpayers who file separately are taxed at the 28% rate once income exceeds $14,875, half the income at which the 28% bracket begins for joint filers.

Single people

Single people have always paid more tax on the same amount of income than married people. Tax reform didn't change that. Starting in 1988, for a single person the 15% rate applies to taxable income only up to $17,850 (compared to $29,750 for married people). The 28% rate applies to taxable income over $17,850.

Heads of households

"Heads of households"—single parents, in plain English—are taxed somewhere between married people and single people. For them, the 15% rate applies to taxable income up to $23,900. The 28% rate becomes effective once taxable income exceeds $23,900.

The secret bracket

It seems simple. It was meant to be simple. But it's not quite that simple. Because, starting in 1988, there's actually a *third tax bracket*. A 33% bracket. Only it's not called a 33% bracket. It's called a "phase-out of the 15% bracket." This secret 33% bracket applies to people with relatively high income.

For married people filing joint returns, the third bracket starts at taxable income of more than $71,900. Married people with taxable income of over $71,900 will first figure out their tax liability using the 15% and 28% brackets. Having determined their tax under those two brackets, they will then increase their tax by 5% of their taxable income between $71,900 and $149,250. Therefore, a couple with $81,900 of taxable income, using the 15% and 28% brackets, will determine that their tax is $19,065 (15% × $29,750 + 28% ($81,900 – $29,750)). They will then add 5% of $10,000 ($81,900 – $71,900), or $500, for a total tax bill of $19,565.

The reason they must add $500 to their tax bill is that Congress decided that people who make a lot of money should have less of their income taxed at the 15% bracket—and the more money they make, Congress decided, the less they should benefit from the 15% bracket. Therefore, for a married couple, once taxable income starts to climb above $71,900, Congress imposes the additional 5% tax and keeps imposing it until income reaches $149,250. By then, it is as though the couple had paid tax on *all* of its income, right from the first dollar, at the 28% rate—that is, the 15% rate never applied to them. In effect, married people with taxable income of $149,250 or more pay a flat tax of 28%.

For single people, this secret 33% bracket first applies at $43,150 of taxable income, and it stays in effect until income reaches $89,560. For heads of households, the 33% bracket first applies at $61,650, and it stays in effect until income reaches $123,790.

THE SECRET THIRD TAX BRACKET STARTING IN 1988

	TAXABLE INCOME	REGULAR TAX	EXTRA SECRET TAX
Single persons	$43,150– 89,560	$ 9,762– 22,757	5% of excess over $43,150
Married couples filing joint returns	71,900– 149,250	16,264– 37,923	5% of excess over $71,900
Heads of households	61,650– 123,790	14,155– 37,923	5% of excess over $61,650

In fact, the secret 33% bracket doesn't even stop at the levels we have indicated above. It goes even higher, and how high depends on how many exemptions you claim. We will return to the secret 33% bracket in Chapter 7.

Is this tax reform?

Note that, under the new tax law, a married couple with taxable income of $30,000 pays tax at the same rates as a couple with $70,000 in taxable income. Before tax reform, the highest rate of tax paid by the $30,000 couple was 25%, while the $70,000 couple paid tax at rates as high as 42%. Which is the fairer system? Surely the $70,000 couple can afford to pay a higher percentage of its income in taxes than the $30,000 couple. Before the tax bill was enacted, there was a good deal of debate over which system was fairer—but eventually the congressmen who thought that people should pay taxes based on what they could afford lost out to the congressmen who thought that progressiveness in the tax system should be sacrificed for simplicity. Later on, we'll see whether simplicity was really achieved.

What about 1987?

For 1987 only, there are special tax brackets. The reason for these special brackets in 1987 had to do with the amount of revenue the tax bill raised. The tax reform act is supposed to be "revenue-neutral." This means that for every dollar of tax revenue lost because of a new tax benefit (such as lower tax rates), another dollar of tax revenue has to be gained from the repeal of an old tax benefit (such as the state sales tax deduction). As it turned out, if the new tax rates of 15% and 28% became effective in 1987, the tax bill would have lost revenue—it would have reduced taxes more quickly than it raised them. This was not an acceptable state of affairs for a Congress faced with a $170 billion deficit. To

THE FIVE TAX BRACKETS FOR 1987 ONLY

	TAXABLE INCOME		
TAX RATE	MARRIED PEOPLE	SINGLE PEOPLE	HEADS OF HOUSEHOLDS
11%	$0–$3,000	$0–$1,800	$0–$2,500
15%	3,000– 28,000	1,800– 16,800	2,500– 23,000
28%	28,000– 45,000	16,800– 27,000	23,000– 38,000
35%	45,000– 90,000	27,000– 54,000	38,000– 80,000
38.5%	Above $90,000	Above $54,000	Above $80,000

make sure that the tax bill didn't throw the budget out of whack (any more than it already was), Congress phased in the repeal of the tax brackets. Instead of providing two brackets in 1987, it provided *five* brackets. Five brackets were still a big improvement over 14 brackets, and they didn't lose so much money for the government.

The marriage tax

The progressive tax system gave us a phenomenon called the "marriage tax." The marriage tax was a "penalty"—in the form of higher taxes—that single, working people paid by getting married. Before tax reform, single people who lived together each filed a separate tax return, and the income of each was taxed at rates that started at zero and went up gradually through the brackets. If they got married they had to file a joint tax return—and then the income of one spouse was piled on top of the income of the other spouse and was taxed at those higher progressive tax rates.

Prior to tax reform, Congress tried to alleviate this marriage tax penalty by giving a special deduction to working married couples—the deduction was equal to 10% of the income of the lower-paid spouse but it was never greater than $3,000. It was called the "deduction for married couples where both spouses work." With the repeal of the tax brackets, Congress decided that the marriage tax penalty had been eliminated. So it *repealed* the "deduction for married couples where both spouses work." This deduction no longer applies after 1986.

But has the penalty been eliminated? Not exactly. Under tax reform, two single people living together, each with a taxable income of $20,000, pay a total of $6,559 in taxes. If they get married, their tax on a joint return would be $7,333. Marriage would cost these people $774. This marriage tax is most likely to affect middle-income people—people who, by getting married and combining their income, are thereby leaving the 15% bracket and entering the 28% bracket. Then why did Congress repeal the "deduction for married couples where both spouses work"? Because, by doing so, it was able to reduce the federal deficit by almost *$27 billion* over the next 5 years.

INCOME AVERAGING

If you have used income averaging in the past, you know what an important tax benefit it has been. Income averaging has enabled you to reduce your taxes in a year with unusually high income by pretending that you earned that income gradually over earlier years. The income averaging rules helped keep income out of the higher tax brackets. If you don't know what income averaging is, don't worry about it. Under tax reform income averaging is repealed, starting in 1987.

DOES ALL OF THIS AMOUNT TO A TAX CUT?

Whether the repeal of the tax brackets cuts your taxes depends on how much money you make and on how many deductions you lost because of tax reform.

Take our couple with $40,000 in taxable income. Before tax reform, their tax liability was $7,435. In 1988, under the new tax brackets their tax liability will be $7,333—a tax savings, under tax reform, of $102. But this assumes that in 1988 this couple still has taxable income of only $40,000. Let's assume that, through some magical process, this couple's earnings do not increase in 1988 and yet their taxable income increases by $2,000. They would then add $560 to their tax bill of $7,333 ($2,000 × 28%). Because of this magical process, their tax is now higher than it was before tax reform. Assuming that earnings do not increase, what magic makes taxable income go up? *The loss of deductions.* As you read on, compare the deductions you've lost with the benefits that you've gained, and then decide whether tax reform cuts your taxes or raises them.

Turning to taxable income

How much tax you pay depends not only on the rates of tax that apply but also on the amount of your taxable income. How you calculate your taxable income, therefore, is just as important as the rates that apply to that income. In the tax reform act, Congress made a great many changes that affect the amount of your taxable income, and it is to those changes that we now direct our fire. Your goal is to keep your taxable income low—and tax reform has made that more difficult to do.

CHAPTER TWO

EXCLUSIONS FROM INCOME

In the tax law, when you ask "What do I have to pay tax on?" or "What is included in my income for tax purposes?," the answer is simple. *Everything.* The tax code says, "Gross income means all income from whatever source derived." Your salary, interest from your savings account, dividends on your stock, your gains from the sale of property, money that you win in the lottery or rob from a bank—it's all income subject to the income tax. Right?

Not quite. There are exceptions. The tax code actually says, *"Except as otherwise provided,* gross income means all income from whatever source derived." And, in fact, the code does provide otherwise. It contains a list of certain kinds of income that are *not* included in income—that actually are *excluded* from income. Under tax reform, this list of exclusions got shorter. Fewer kinds of income are excluded from income after tax reform than before it.

First, the good news. There were many exclusions from income that Congress might have taken away but didn't. For example, if your employer provides medical insurance for you, you don't pay taxes on the value of that benefit. Those medical insurance premiums that he pays every month on your behalf are *excluded* from your gross income. Congress considered repealing this exclusion, but voted to retain it. Some other common exclusions from income that are still in the law:

★ life insurance proceeds that you receive when someone dies who named you as beneficiary

★ damages you receive from a personal injury lawsuit

★ the money you receive from your health insurance company to pay your medical bills

★ gifts that you receive or money that you inherit

★ premiums paid by your employer on the first $50,000 of term insurance on your life

★ a variety of "fringe benefits" or "perquisites" ("perks") that your employer may provide to you and your fellow employees

★ interest that you earn on tax-exempt state and local government bonds

The above items, and many other more esoteric ones, are still excluded from gross income.

Now, the bad news. The following exclusions from income have been repealed.

The $200 dividend exclusion

Until tax reform, you excluded from income the first $100 in dividends that you received on your stock holdings, and married people filing joint returns could exclude $200 in dividends. Not any more. This exclusion is repealed, starting in 1987. All dividends that you receive on your stock after December 31, 1986, are taxed.

Scholarships and fellowships

Before tax reform if you (or your child) were studying toward a degree, all scholarship money that you received for tuition, room and board, for travel, books, research, and equipment was excluded from income. It was tax-free money.

But not any more. Under tax reform, scholarship money for tuition and for course-related expenses such as books, supplies, and equipment, will still be excluded if you are working toward a degree. But scholarship money for room and board and incidental expenses will be taxable. For the coveted athlete who gets a penthouse, a car, and $1,000 per week in laundry money, taxable income can start to mount up pretty quickly, and he may have to go to work in the summer just to pay his taxes. Before tax reform, degree candidates who were required to teach courses or run labs as part of their curriculum (usually post-graduates), and who were paid for that work, did not have to pay taxes on that income, either. Under tax reform, however, that money will also be taxed.

Before tax reform, people who were not studying toward a degree could exclude up to $10,800 for tuition and room and board, as long as the money came from a tax-exempt organization. And there was no limit on the exclusion for incidental expenses. Under tax reform, the exclusion for scholarships and fellowships for non-degree candidates is repealed entirely. All the money they receive for their education will be taxed. However, the tax reform bill appears to broaden the circumstances under which you will be viewed as working toward a degree. According to the explanation of the tax reform act supplied by the Congress (this explanation is called the Conference Report), you are working toward a degree if you are enrolled in an institution that offers a program that is acceptable for full credit toward a degree. The Conference Report appears to state that you are working toward a degree (and your scholarship for tuition and course-related expenses is therefore excluded from income) no matter how slowly you are working toward it. You don't have to be a full-time student to qualify for the scholarship exclusion. The repeal of the exclusion for non-degree candidates, therefore, is aimed at the fellowship people who spend some time at an institution in a special course of study which cannot possibly result in a degree. The Conference Report also makes it clear that scholarships for study at vocational schools are excluded from income as long as you have embarked on a course of study that will qualify you for a job.

The new rules on scholarships and fellowships apply starting on January 1, 1987. However, they do not apply at all to scholarships or fellowships granted before August 17, 1986, regardless of when the money is received. Scholarships granted on or after August 17, 1986 will still be tax free if they are received before January 1, 1987 to defray expenses incurred before that date (such as room and board expenses incurred before January 1, 1987). But all amounts received on or after January 1, 1987 from scholarships granted on or after August 17, 1986 are subject to the new rules.

Unemployment compensation

Before tax reform, a portion of—and sometimes all—state or federal unemployment compensation was excluded from income. Starting in 1987, all state and federal unemployment compensation will be taxed.

Some highly paid corporate executives purchase private unemployment insurance—insurance which usually pays them benefits if they are fired after a corporate take-over. Unemployment pay from a private insurance contract is still excluded from income.

Prizes and awards

Did you know that all the money people received when they won the Nobel Prize or the Pulitzer Prize was tax-free? So was prize money for other "literary" or "artistic" or "civic" achievements. Before tax reform it was excluded from income. But not anymore. Achievement awards granted after 1986 are taxable. There's only one exception: the exclusion still applies for people who donate their prize money to charity. (Prizes and awards from contests that you enter—like lottery drawings or television game shows—have always been taxable.)

Big companies like to give their employees awards for a variety of reasons—it's a way to compensate people tax-free for doing good work. Under tax reform, the exclusions for these awards are also repealed—except for length-of-service awards and job-safety awards within certain limits. Awards of minimal value—such as traditional retirement gifts—will remain tax-free.

SUMMARY

After tax reform you will total up your gross income just as you did before tax reform. Everything that was income before tax reform is still income after tax reform and, except for the items listed above, everything that was excluded from income before tax reform is still excluded. So if you were receiving a certain kind of income that you know was not taxable, and you ask, "Is this income still tax-free?", the answer is probably "Yes," unless it is one of the items we've just discussed.

CHAPTER THREE

ITEMIZED DEDUCTIONS

After you figure out your gross income (including in income everything that isn't specifically excluded), you can start to reduce your gross income by your deductions in order to arrive at your taxable income. There are two broad categories of deductions: business deductions and personal or "itemized" deductions. When you do your tax return, your business deductions are subtracted first to arrive at your "adjusted gross income"—the figure that you fill in at the bottom of the front page of IRS Form 1040 for 1986. Then the itemized deductions are subtracted from adjusted gross income to arrive at taxable income. However, even though itemized deductions are subtracted last, we will look at tax reform changes in itemized deductions first because then it will be easier to understand the changes in the business deductions.

Not everybody claims itemized deductions. Some people claim the standard deduction instead, and we will discuss the standard deduction in the next chapter. One of Congress's goals in enacting the tax reform bill was to make more people use the "short form" (Form 1040A) in filling out their tax returns. You can't use the short form if you claim itemized deductions. So, as we will see, Congress raised the standard deduction to make it more attractive to a greater number of people. And not only did Congress use a carrot in the form of a higher standard deduction to get you to use the short form, it also used a stick. It repealed or limited some of the itemized deductions. Congress no doubt had good intentions with all these changes but, for the short term, at least, the changes will probably cause a great deal of confusion. Until tax reform, most people had a fairly good understanding of whether they should itemize deductions or just claim the standard deduction. Now, with the higher standard deduction and the loss of some itemized deductions, many people may be unsure. For a couple of years at least, they will have to fill out the long form (Form 1040) in order to determine whether the short form is all they need to use.

MEDICAL EXPENSES

Before tax reform, medical expenses—all the money you spend on doctors, dentists, hospitals, pharmaceuticals, and medical insurance—were deductible to the extent they exceeded 5% of your adjusted gross income. You added up your medical expenses, you took 5% of your adjusted gross income, and the difference between the two figures was your medical expense deduction. Under tax reform, starting with your 1987 return, medical expenses are deductible to the extent they exceed 7½% of your adjusted gross income. Therefore, a smaller amount of medical expenses is deductible. If your adjusted gross income in 1987 is $30,000, only medical expenses in excess of $2,250 are deductible (compared to $1,500 in 1986). If your adjusted gross income in 1987 is $60,000, only medical expenses in excess of $4,500 are deductible (compared to $3,000 in 1986).

While the tax reform act makes it more difficult for people in general to claim a deduction for medical expenses, it also gives a break to self-employed people for certain medical expenses. Under tax reform, starting in 1987, self-employed people can claim a deduction *from gross income* for 25% of amounts that they pay for medical insurance for themselves and their families. (The remaining 75% is an itemized deduction subject to the 7½% floor.) In general, their health insurance plans must also cover their employees, and the amount of the deduction claimed under this rule cannot exceed their earned income from self-employment. Also, this deduction from gross income is not allowed if a self-employed person is also employed by someone else and is eligible to participate on a subsidized basis in a health plan of that employer (or in the plan of the employer of his spouse). The new deduction for self-employed people is intended to give them a tax benefit comparable to that enjoyed by employees who receive health insurance coverage tax-free.

TAXES

Income taxes that you pay to your state or city are still deductible.

Property taxes—real property or personal property—are still deductible.

Sales taxes that you pay after 1986 are no longer deductible. The deduction for sales taxes is repealed. But if you pay sales taxes on big-ticket items that are likely to increase in value—like building materials for your home, or jewelry or art—don't throw away the sales tax receipt. When you go to sell that property, the sales tax that you paid will be added to the cost of the property and will reduce the amount of your taxable profit.

INTEREST

Prior to tax reform, most interest that you paid was deductible if you itemized deductions. There were always limitations on deducting interest that you paid on money borrowed to make investments—a subject we will cover in Chapter 14—but apart from those limitations virtually all interest was deductible. With tax reform, that is no longer the case.

Home mortgage interest

Interest that you pay on your home mortgage is still deductible. So is interest that you pay on a mortgage on your vacation home. But two homes is the limit. If you have two vacation homes in addition to your primary residence, interest paid on a mortgage on one of those vacation homes is not deductible as an itemized deduction (it may be deductible as interest on investment property—to be covered later on). You can choose which vacation home you want to claim itemized interest deductions from. Now suppose you don't have a mortgage on your primary residence but you have two vacation homes and both are mortgaged. It's time to refinance your real properties. You can claim interest as an itemized deduction on only one of those vacation homes.

The "purchase price rule"

Although a deduction for home mortgage interest is still allowed, there is a limit to how much home mortgage interest you can deduct. Under the "purchase price rule," only interest on that part of the mortgage that doesn't exceed the original purchase price of your home, plus the cost of improvements, is deductible. If you bought your home for $100,000 and it carries a $90,000 mortgage, all the interest is deductible. But if your home has appreciated in value to $200,000 and you refinance it with a $150,000 mortgage, only two-thirds ($100,000/$150,000) of the interest on the $150,000 mortgage is deductible. The interest on the $50,000 portion of the new mortgage that exceeds the original cost of your home may not be claimed. If you were a savvy real estate buyer who paid $100,000 several years ago for a home that is worth $1,000,000 today, the tax law has turned against you. You can borrow $900,000 on your home if you want to—but only the interest on the first $100,000 of that loan will be deductible. There are two exceptions to this "purchase price rule." Under one exception, if the proceeds of any portion of a mortgage that exceeds the purchase price of your home are used to pay for education expenses for you or your children, or for medical bills, interest on that portion of your mortgage is deductible even though the mortgage violates the purchase price rule. So if you refinanced your $100,000 home for $150,000, and used $30,000 of the proceeds to pay education expenses, or medical bills, you can deduct interest on $130,000 of the mortgage.

The second exception to the "purchase price rule" is a "grandfather" rule. If you took out a loan on your home on or before August 16, 1986, then all of the interest on that loan is deductible even if the amount of the loan exceeds what you paid for the house. Only interest on home mortgages taken out after August 16, 1986, is subject to the purchase price rule.

Why did Congress limit home mortgage interest deductions in this manner? Read the next paragraph.

Consumer interest is no longer deductible, starting in 1987. Interest that you pay on your car loan (if you don't use your car in your business), on your credit card balances or on other loans you've taken out for personal reasons is consumer interest and is disallowed. Congress dreamed up the "purchase price rule" for interest on home mortgages partly out of a fear that everyone would refinance their homes to pay off their consumer debt. Congress figured people would simply convert consumer interest into home mortgage interest, and thereby continue to deduct all the interest they deducted before tax reform. This was clever thinking on the part of Congress but, still, it may have overreacted.

Note that interest on an education loan is consumer interest and is not deductible, unless the loan is secured by a mortgage on your home (or vacation home). It seems unfair that you have to mortgage your home just to deduct the interest on an education loan, but that is what the law says. Note also that interest you pay to the IRS on a tax deficiency is also consumer interest. *All* interest is consumer interest unless it's interest on a home mortgage or on a loan taken out for your business or investments.

Interest on loans that you take out for your business is always deductible (and is claimed on a different schedule than Schedule A). Interest on borrowings for investments may or may not be deductible, depending on how well you invest. We'll cover this problem later.

Interest deduction rules are phased in

Some people may think that it is unfair for consumer interest to be suddenly nondeductible after they have run up large amounts of consumer debt believing that they could deduct the interest on their debts. Congress anticipated that grievance, and the new rules that disallow deductions for consumer interest, home mortgage interest that violates the purchase price rule, and investment interest (to be covered later) don't become effective all at once. They become effective *gradually,* to give you time to pay off your debts. In 1987, you can still deduct 65% of the consumer interest that you pay in that year. In 1988, you can deduct 40% of the consumer interest that you pay. In 1989, 20%, and in 1990, 10% of your consumer interest will be deductible. No consumer interest will be deductible in 1991 and thereafter.

CONSUMER INTEREST—GOING, GOING . . . GONE!		
Percentage of consumer interest deduction allowed on your income tax, by year		
1986–100%	1988–40%	1990–10%
1987– 65%	1989–20%	1991– 0%

The same phase-in rule applies to home mortgage interest that violates the "purchase price rule": 65% of that interest will still be allowed in 1987, 40% in 1988, and so on until 1991 when none of it will be allowed.

CHARITABLE CONTRIBUTION DEDUCTIONS

Congress didn't make any changes in the deductibility of charitable contributions for people who itemize deductions. The charitable contribution deduction for people who *don't* itemize deductions has always been scheduled to expire after 1986, and in fact it will. But for itemizers there are no changes in the general rules for charitable contributions (people who donate appreciated property to charities should consult their tax advisors).

CASUALTY LOSSES

You can claim an itemized deduction for losses to your property which you suffer due to "fire, storm, shipwreck, or other casualty, or from theft." Casualty losses above $100 are deductible to the extent that they exceed 10% of your adjusted gross income. If you are insured against a loss, the amount of any loss must be reduced by the insurance proceeds that you collect.

The IRS has always taken the position that, if you do have insurance, then you must file a claim under your insurance policy and either reduce the amount of the loss by the insurance payment or show that the claim was denied. However, in many casualties, particularly automobile or boating accidents, people choose not to file a claim out of fear that their insurance premiums will go up. Without insurance reimbursement, the amount of the casualty loss deduction is greater than it would otherwise be. On several occasions the IRS disallowed casualty loss deductions of people who hadn't filed insurance claims, but in nearly every case the courts held that filing an insurance claim was not a prerequisite to claiming a casualty loss deduction.

The IRS ran to Congress for help and got it in the tax reform act. Any insured casualty loss suffered after 1985 is deductible only if an insurance claim has been filed.

MISCELLANEOUS ITEMIZED DEDUCTIONS

The deductions listed above—as well as certain special itemized deductions—are the major itemized deductions. The "miscellaneous itemized deductions" are all the other deductions that are allowed if you itemize deductions. They include the following: union dues and certain other expenses you incur in your employment; tax-return preparation fees or the cost of tax advice; money that you lose on a transaction entered into for profit; expenses that you pay in connection with your investment (as opposed to your business) activities, such as broker's fees or investment magazine subscriptions. There are other miscellaneous itemized deductions that are more esoteric. And there will be still more miscellaneous itemized deductions because, as we shall soon see, some deductions that in the past could be claimed *regardless* of whether you itemized deductions will, under tax reform, be allowed *only* if you itemize deductions, and then only as miscellaneous itemized deductions.

And now for the bad news. In the past, the miscellaneous itemized deductions were allowable in full just like the other itemized deductions; but starting in 1987 your miscellaneous itemized deductions will be allowed only to the extent that they exceed 2% of your adjusted gross income. It's the same sort of rule that applies to medical expense deductions, but with a 2% floor rather than a 7½% floor.

As we go through the tax reform bill, we are going to see more miscellaneous itemized deductions that become subject to this 2% rule. So we will set up a "2% pot" for these deductions that we will drag out from time to time whenever we have another miscellaneous itemized deduction to put into it.

Those are the tax-reform changes that apply to most of the itemized deductions, but we will pick up some stragglers later on. If you are wondering whether one of your favorite itemized deductions can still be claimed after tax reform, the answer is "Yes," unless it is covered by one of the changes described above.

CHAPTER FOUR

WHAT HAPPENED TO THE ZERO BRACKET AMOUNT?

For generations, when people figured out their income tax and didn't itemize their deductions, they reduced their adjusted gross income by the "standard deduction." For non-itemizers, it was just a straight reduction in the amount of income subject to tax. Everybody knew what the "standard deduction" was. It was practically an American institution. Then, in 1977, Congress eliminated the standard deduction and replaced it with, of all things, the "zero bracket amount." The zero bracket amount did exactly the same thing that the standard deduction did—it reduced your adjusted gross income—but you couldn't *see* it. When you had claimed the standard deduction on your tax return, you actually subtracted the amount of the standard deduction from your adjusted gross income. The zero bracket amount, on the other hand, was not subtracted from adjusted gross income. It was built into the tax brackets and reduced your income automatically: if your adjusted gross income was $30,000, the tax tables gave you a tax liability that was based on an amount equal to $30,000 *minus* the zero bracket amount.

The elimination of the standard deduction in 1977 was met with both outrage and consternation. Thousands of people called the IRS or their tax advisors to ask: "What happened to the standard deduction? Where's the reduction in income that I get every year?"

By 1986, taxpayers had learned that the zero bracket amount did everything that the standard deduction did, and they had grown accustomed to it. So what did Congress do? It repealed the zero bracket amount and resurrected the standard deduction! Starting in 1987 you must *claim* the standard deduction once again. It's no longer built into the tax brackets. You must once again perform the arithmetical function of subtracting the standard deduction from your adjusted gross income. Don't overlook it! And if you call the IRS to ask, "What's this standard deduction all about?" they will know that you didn't file a tax return before 1978.

How much is the resurrected standard deduction worth? This part is easy:

THE NEW STANDARD DEDUCTION

INCOME TAX FILING STATUS	1986 ZERO-BRACKET DEDUCTION	1987 STANDARD DEDUCTION	1988 STANDARD DEDUCTION
Joint returns (and surviving spouses)	$3,540	$3,760	$5,000
Heads of households	2,390	2,540	4,400
Single taxpayers	2,390	2,540	3,000
Married filing separately	1,770	1,880	2,500

Period. Well, almost. The standard deduction will be increased for inflation starting in 1989. So if inflation during 1988 runs at 5%, the standard deduction for 1989 will be 5% greater—for joint returns, for example, it would be $5,250.

The standard deduction for elderly people (age 65 or over) and for blind people is higher. For people who are either elderly or blind, the higher standard deduction figures for 1988 apply in 1987 as well. Also, a single person (other than a surviving spouse) who is elderly or blind can claim an additional standard deduction of $750— and $1,500 if he is elderly *and* blind. A married person who is elderly or blind can claim an additional standard deduction of $600, or $1,200 if he is both. These additional standard deduction amounts apply for both 1987 and 1988, and will be adjusted for inflation after 1988.

CHAPTER FIVE

BUSINESS MEALS AND ENTERTAINMENT EXPENSES

Deductions for the cost of business meals and entertainment have always been controversial. As long ago as 1961, President John Kennedy said that it was time for the Congress to do something about these deductions which effectively make the government pay for a part of a businessman's lunches and theatre tickets. Twenty-five years later Congress responded. Kennedy had said that "too many firms and individuals have devised means of deducting too many personal living expenses as business expenses, thereby charging a large part of their cost to the Federal Government. . . . This is a matter of national concern, affecting not only our public revenues, our sense of fairness, and our respect for the tax system, but our moral and business practices as well."

"We agree!" the Congress finally said in 1986. And it promptly disallowed all of 20% of the cost of a business meal or an entertainment expense. This seems like a slap on the wrist for an evil of "national concern" that affects our "moral practices," but that is what the Congress did. Starting in 1987, only 80% of the cost of business meals and entertainment is deductible.

Whose expenses are we talking about?

Let's clarify that first. Your employer may give you an expense account which you use to take customers or clients to lunch. You pay for the meal and then you are reimbursed. When that happens, we are talking about your employer's expenses. If you are reimbursed, for you the whole transaction is a wash, and you don't benefit from a deduction. In these circumstances, it is your employer who, under tax reform, can claim only 80% of the cost of the meal. If you pay $100 for a business lunch and your employer reimburses you, he can now deduct only $80.

Sometimes, however, your employer doesn't reimburse you. Instead, he pays you a generous salary and expects you to wine and dine customers out of that. When your employer pays you a generous salary which includes a wining and dining allowance, he deducts all the money he pays you because he lists it all as salary, not partly as salary and partly as meal or entertainment expenses. It is now you who must deduct the portion of that salary spent on meal and entertainment expenses, and you are the one who, under tax reform, can deduct only $80 of a $100 meal. Don't be surprised if, after tax reform, your employer decides to increase your salary and let you be responsible for your own business meal and entertainment expenses.

The bad news for employees

If your employer doesn't reimburse you and you wine and dine customers out of your salary, you're in for an unpleasant surprise. When you are employed by someone else, the business meal or entertainment expense deduction is an itemized deduction (and it always has been). In fact, it is a *miscellaneous* itemized deduction. Do you remember what happened to miscellaneous itemized deductions? Starting in 1987, they are deductible only to the extent they exceed 2% of your adjusted gross income. Bring out the 2% pot! Note the double limitation on these deductions that results. First, you can list only 80% of a business meal or entertainment expense as an itemized deduction. Second, you can actually deduct it only to the extent that, together with the rest of your miscellaneous itemized deductions, it exceeds 2% of your adjusted gross income. If you spend $2,000 in a year on business meals and have an adjusted gross income of $70,000 (and no other miscellaneous itemized deductions), your allowable deduction for business meals is $200. Only $1,600 of the expenses (80% of $2,000) can be claimed in the first place, and of that $1,600, only the portion above $1,400 (2% of $70,000) can actually be deducted. So be sure to negotiate with your employer for an expense account. If you account for your own business meal expenses, the new rules hurt you more than they hurt your employer.

DOUBLE LIMITATION ON THE THREE-MARTINI LUNCH	
Businessman's adjusted gross income	$70,000
Expenses for business meals	2,000
80% income tax deduction for business meals	1,600
Less 2% of adjusted gross income	1,400
Total deduction allowed for business meals	200

If you are your own employer—that is, if you are self-employed—then you still claim the deduction, and lose 20% of it, but you claim it on Schedule C of Form 1040 (sole proprietorship) or perhaps on a partnership tax return that you file with your partner.

New requirements for claiming business meal deductions

Before tax reform, there were differences in the requirements for deducting an entertainment expense and for deducting a business meal expense. The rules on entertainment expenses have always been stricter. One way to claim an entertainment expense is to show that the entertainment was "directly related" to the active conduct of your business. An expense is "directly related" if a business meeting occurs during the entertainment period—for example, you negotiate a contract while you play golf or while you're fishing. An expense is also a "directly related" expense if the entertainment occurs in a clear business setting—for example, to generate publicity for a new business you have a cocktail party for all the important people in town.

If you can't show that the entertainment is "directly related" to the active conduct of your business, then you must show that the entertainment occurred just before or just after a business discussion, and that it was "associated with" the conduct of your business. This kind of entertainment is usually goodwill. No business is discussed during the entertainment, but business was discussed just before it or is to be discussed just after it. For example, you work at the office with your client all day, and then you take him to the theatre. The cost of the theatre tickets—after tax reform, 80% of the total cost—is deductible as an entertainment expense because it is "associated with" the conduct of your business.

Also, deductions for entertainment expenses have always required more substantiation than deductions for business meals. In order to claim an entertainment expense, you have to show— usually with receipts, diaries, or other documentary evidence—the amount of the expense, the time and place the entertainment took place, the business purpose of the expense, and the business relationship to you of the person you entertained. And you need a receipt for any expense over $25.

Before tax reform, none of these rules applied to *business meals*. A deduction was allowed if a business meal simply took place in an atmosphere *conducive* to a business discussion. All that meant was that there couldn't be so much distraction that it was impossible to discuss business. The cost of a meal at a nightclub, for example, or at the race track, wasn't deductible because that was entertainment and had to pass the "associated with" test. But the cost of any meal at a restaurant was deductible. You didn't have to discuss business, you could talk about the moon. As long as the person you were with was a customer or client, or a prospective customer or client, or even just a colleague whom you consulted with, the cost of the meal was deductible. The business meal deduction, in effect, could be a deduction solely for the cost of goodwill. Also, the substantiation requirements for business meals were not so onerous.

Not any more, however. After tax reform, business meals must pass the same tests as entertainment expenses. Starting in 1987, such meals must be "directly connected" with the conduct of your business or "associated with" it. Business must be discussed during the meal, or the meal must occur just before or just after a business meeting. And the business meal expense must be substantiated in the same manner as an entertainment expense. Otherwise, no deduction.

The "lavish and extravagant" problem

The law has always disallowed "lavish or extravagant" business meal and entertainment expenses that you incurred while traveling on business. The tax reform act contains a specific provision prohibiting deductions for all lavish or extravagant business meal or entertainment expenses, whether or not incurred while in a travel status. What, exactly, is "lavish or extravagant" has never been clear. A $150 bill for dinner for two in Manhattan is clearly not extravagant. But spending $150 for dinner in a small, desert town in Arizona might be outrageous. Lavishness or extravagance may be like pornography—you know it when you see it.

Investment-purpose meals

Before tax reform, if you incurred a meal or entertainment expense in connection with your investment activities—as opposed to your business activities—the expense was fully deductible as an itemized deduction. For example, if you took a gold guru to dinner, hoping to get a buy or sell signal, or if you had a drink with your stockbroker and picked up the tab, you could claim a deduction for that. But not any more. Under tax reform, business meal and entertainment expenses are deductible only if they are related to a business activity, not if they are related to your investments.

All of the business meal and entertainment expense rules apply to expenses incurred after 1986.

CHAPTER SIX

TRAVEL AND TRANSPORTATION EXPENSES

At the beginning of Chapter 3 we saw that there were two broad categories of deductions—business deductions and itemized deductions. Business deductions, we said, were deductible from gross income to arrive at adjusted gross income. We were referring mostly to travel and entertainment expenses, although there are other business deductions, too, and we shall get to them in due course. Travel and transportation expenses *were* deductible from gross income, but that was before the tax act of 1986.

A "travel expense" is an expense that you incur while you are away from home on business. Travel expenses include the cost of the transportation to get to your away-from-home destination, food and lodging costs, and incidental expenses such as dry cleaning or calls back home. You are "away from home"—and, therefore, incurring travel expenses—if you travel to a destination outside the metropolitan area where you *work* (not outside the area where you reside) and if you remain there overnight (or at least for a long enough time to require some rest before you return). If you work in Manhattan and travel to Brooklyn on business and spend the night there, you are not away from home. But an overnight business trip to New Haven, Connecticut would put you in a travel status under the tax law.

A "transportation" expense, under the tax law, refers to the cost of *local* transportation. A taxi-fare downtown or the subway fare, and the cost of parking your car while on business around town or the cost of gas and tolls, are all transportation costs under the tax law. Once you start to head away from home, the cost of getting there—i.e., the long distance transportation cost—becomes a travel expense.

THE IRS SAYS TRANSPORTATION COSTS ARE NOT TRAVEL EXPENSES

TRANSPORTATION COSTS

All *local* transportation expenses such as:
Taxi, bus, and subway fare in home city
Car parking fees
Gasoline costs
Toll bridge fees

TRAVEL EXPENSES

All business costs incurred away from home such as—
Air and train fares
Food and lodging costs
Dry cleaning expense
Cost of telephone calls home
Transportation costs away from home

As with business meals and entertainment expenses, if you are employed you might pay for travel and transportation expenses and receive reimbursement under an expense account arrangement, or you might pay for these expenses out of your salary. As with business meals and entertainment expenses, the arrangement you have with your employer determines how much the tax reform act affects you.

Transportation expenses

Prior to the new tax act, if you paid transportation expenses in connection with your job (other than commuting expenses) and did not get reimbursed, you could claim a deduction for these expenses *regardless of whether you itemized deductions.* You used the expense to reduce gross income to adjusted gross income. Under tax reform, these expenses become itemized deductions. Starting in 1987, you can claim them only if you itemize. And not only do they become itemized deductions, they become *miscellaneous* itemized deductions—deductible only to the extent that, together with your other miscellaneous itemized deductions, they exceed 2% of your adjusted gross income. So bring out the 2% pot.

Before tax reform, if your transportation expenses related to your investments, rather than to your business, they were always deductible—but only as itemized deductions. The only difference under tax reform is that they get thrown into the 2% pot.

If you are self-employed, your transportation expenses are fully deductible on your self-employment schedule (Schedule C of Form 1040 for sole proprietorships), or on a partnership return.

Travel expenses

Tax reform has made a number of changes in the travel expense rules.

First, if you eat a meal while away from home on business, that is a travel expense. But under tax reform *only 80% of the cost of meals while traveling is deductible.* The rules that now apply to business meals and entertainment expenses also apply to meals that you buy while traveling. So if you are in a distant city, all by yourself, eating a lousy meal in a dumpy restaurant while wishing you were home, only 80% of the cost of the meal is deductible. Congress does not explain why it extended the 80% rule to meals while you are in a travel status. The perceived evil is the deductible $100 business lunch eaten right across the street from your office, compared to the nondeductible $3.95 sandwich eaten in your office. Perhaps Congress thought that most meals away from home would be eaten with a business colleague anyway and should therefore be subject to the business meals rule. Maybe Congressmen never dine alone, but businessmen know better.

Remember that the strict substantiation requirements of entertainment expenses now apply to business meals, including meals consumed while in a travel status. However, if you do dine alone while traveling, obviously you don't have to establish the business purpose of the meal if you have already established the business purpose of the trip, or the business relationship to your nonexistent guest.

Second, all unreimbursed travel expenses paid by you as an employee, which were once deductible regardless of whether you itemized deductions, are now, like transportation expenses, miscellaneous itemized deductions. Bring out the 2% pot. (Performing artists may still deduct travel expenses regardless of whether they itemize deductions and their expenses, therefore, are not subject to the 2% pot.)

Third, deductions for *luxury water travel* are severely limited. If you plan to attend a business meeting in London or Caracas, and you decide to go there by ocean liner, you will no longer be permitted to deduct the entire cost of the crossing. Instead, your deduction will be determined under a formula: the number of days of passage times twice the highest per diem travel allowance for Federal Government employees. In 1986, the highest per diem travel allowance for government employees was about $75. So if your New York–London passage took 5 days, your maximum deduction for the cost of transportation to London would be $5 \times \$75 \times 2 = \$750$.

Seminars and conventions

Before the 1986 tax act, when you attended a seminar or convention, you claimed a deduction for all the travel expenses you paid to go there plus any attendance fee that you paid. If the seminar or convention was related to your trade or business—such as a lawyers' convention or a seminar on new products for life insurance salesmen—you deducted the cost of the meeting regardless of whether you itemized deductions. If it was an investment seminar that you attended in order to learn how to better manage your portfolio, you claimed the travel expenses and the attendance fee as an itemized deduction.

The IRS has always claimed that the expenses of attending a seminar or convention are deductible only if the meeting is related to your trade or business. The cost of "investment seminars," the Service says, is not deductible. That may or may not be true for investment seminars attended before tax reform, and someday a court will no doubt decide whether the cost of attending pre-tax reform investment seminars is deductible. The 1986 tax act, however, states quite clearly that no deduction is allowed for travel expenses or attendance fees for investment seminars. Under tax reform, the seminar or convention must be related to your business if the cost of attending it is to be deductible. The Conference Report, which explained the tax act and was submitted with the bill, also states that no deduction is to be allowed even for business seminars or meetings if the entire meeting is on videotapes which you view at your leisure in your hotel room. The Congress apparently suspects that these kinds of seminars are vacations in disguise. The tax reform act itself does not contain this provision, but this is what Congress understands the law to be.

Also—you guessed it—travel expenses and attendance fees for seminars and conventions, even though business related, are now claimed as *miscellaneous itemized deductions*. Bring out the 2% pot!

Travel as a form of education
Education expenses are generally deductible if the education improves your skills at your job or is required by your employer in order to keep your job. That was true before tax reform and it

is still true. For some people, however, travel itself became a form of education. For example, a high school teacher who taught French took a sabbatical to travel through France, visited French schools, went to French movies and plays, and attended lectures in the French language. She claimed a deduction for the cost of the entire trip because it improved her skills as a French teacher. Or an ancient history professor would travel to Greece and Egypt to get a better feel for the places he talked about in his classes, so he deducted the trip as an education expense.

Not any more. Under tax reform, no deduction is allowed for the cost of travel as a form of education.

Charitable travel

A deduction has always been allowed for travel expenses which you incur while working for a charity. This deduction was frequently abused. On Friday you would travel to Denver on behalf of a charity, do your charitable work during the afternoon, then hop over to Vail for the weekend. You would deduct the cost of the airfare to Denver and back. Under tax reform, deductions for charitable travel expenses are allowed only if the travel involves no significant element of recreation. This rule is the same one that has always applied to deductible medical travel expenses.

All of the tax reform changes in travel deductions apply starting in 1987.

MOVING EXPENSES

Moving expenses may seem personal in nature, but Congress once thought that in this country moving was a cost of earning money. Congress also once said that a mobile labor force was important to the economy. Consequently, moving expenses, to the extent deductible, were always deductible from gross income to arrive at adjusted gross income.

Tax reform has changed that. Starting with 1987, moving expenses are an itemized deduction. Do we need the 2% pot? No. Moving expenses are not a miscellaneous itemized deduction. They are fully deductible if you itemize deductions.

IRA's

Individual retirement account contributions have always been deductible from gross income, but after tax reform they are deductible only under certain conditions. We cover IRA's in Chapter 15.

SUMMARY

We have now reviewed all the changes of general application made in business deductions by the tax reform act. You may have noticed something. Except for IRA's, none of these expenses is still deductible from gross income. They have all become itemized deductions and, except for moving expenses, they all go in the 2% pot. For some people, the 2% pot will be their most important itemized deduction. If you understand politics, you realize that someday Congress may make the 2% pot a 7½% pot, just as it did with medical expenses.

CHAPTER SEVEN

PERSONAL EXEMPTIONS

Affter you have reduced your gross income by your business deductions, which after tax reform are almost all itemized deductions, and by your regular itemized deductions or the standard deduction, you come down to the personal exemptions. The reduction in your income by the amount of your personal exemptions brings you to your taxable income.

The personal exemptions have always been the simplest part of the tax laws. You get an exemption for yourself, you get one for your spouse; you get one exemption for each of your children and other dependents; and you add up your exemptions, multiply the total by the exemption amount for the year, and subtract the product from your income. That's all there is to it. If you claimed four exemptions at $1,080 each on your 1986 tax return, you reduced your income subject to tax by $4,320.

Under the tax reform act, the amount of the personal exemption is going up—way up. In 1987, each exemption is worth $1,900; in 1988, each amounts to $1,950; and in 1989, $2,000. Like the standard deduction, the personal exemption will be adjusted for inflation after 1989.

UP GO THE PERSONAL EXEMPTIONS	
Value of the personal exemption for you and each dependent, by year:	1986—$1,080 1987—$1,900 1988—$1,950 1989—$2,000 1990—$2,000 plus inflation adjustment

That's the good news. Now for the bad news.

Exemptions cannot be claimed by your children

Prior to tax reform, if your child or any other dependent had income of his own—from a trust fund or a savings account—he could claim a personal exemption for himself even if you claimed him as an exemption on your tax return. The practical effect of this benefit was that as long as your child's income didn't exceed $1,080 (in 1986), he didn't have to file a tax return. Starting in 1987, he can't claim his own exemption if you claim an exemption for him.

Does this mean that your child has to file a tax return to report $11.80 in interest from his savings account? Well, do you think all congressmen are crazy? The answer to the first question is "No." Your child still has the standard deduction. Under the old law, the standard deduction—then called the zero bracket amount—could be used only to reduce *earned* income, such as money your child makes on his paper route. The standard deduction could not be used to reduce *passive* income, such as savings account interest. However, in order to prevent 40 million children from filing tax returns to report an average $11.80 in interest, Congress said that, under tax reform, although your child cannot claim a personal exemption, he can use up to $500 of his standard deduction to offset passive income. But if your child's passive income exceeds $500, he has to file a tax return.

Suppose your child has $1,000 in earned income from his paper route, and $600 in interest from his savings account. The standard deduction is $2,540 (in 1987), but he still must file a tax return. He can use $1,000 of his standard deduction to offset the $1,000 in paper-route income, but only $500 of his standard deduction can be applied against the savings account interest. Since he cannot claim a personal exemption, he has taxable income of $100, and owes the government $15. An accountant will charge you only about $250 to prepare his return.

Incidentally, under tax reform, if you claim an

exemption on your tax return for a child over 5 years old, you will have to provide his Social Security number, starting with your 1987 return. Thus your child will have to get a Social Security number after he turns five.

That's the bad news. Now for the *terrible* news.

If you make lots of money, starting in 1988, your personal exemptions won't help you much anyway! Once your taxable income starts to climb past $149,250 if you are married—$89,560 if you are single, and $123,790 if you are a head of household—the value of your personal exemptions will start to go down in 1988. You will continue to claim them, but they won't do you as much good. Why? You may recall that, back in Chapter 1, we discussed the secret 33% bracket that applies to people with high income. This bracket is the one that eventually eliminates the value of the 15% bracket to people whose income exceeds a certain level. For married people, for example, the 33% bracket starts to apply at taxable income of $71,900 and stays in effect until taxable income reaches $149,250, at which point the couple has paid tax on all of its income at the 28% rate. We said in Chapter 1 that actually the 33% bracket didn't stop at $149,250 but went higher, depending on how many exemptions you claim. In fact, this 33% bracket, after eliminating the benefits to you of the 15% bracket, stays in effect and starts to work on the value of your exemptions. It continues to apply until it eliminates any tax savings you would otherwise derive from your personal exemption.

The tax-saving value to you of your personal exemptions is eliminated gradually, just as the value of the 15% bracket was. The value of each exemption that you claim is eliminated over each $10,920 of taxable income. For each exemption claimed, the 33% bracket continues to apply (after it has phased out the 15% bracket) to an additional $10,920 of taxable income. A married couple with no children claims two exemptions on their tax return; therefore, for them the tax benefits of their two exemptions are phased out over $21,840 of taxable income ($10,920 × 2). After the 33% bracket has eliminated the benefit to them of the 15% bracket (at $149,250 of taxable income), it continues to apply over the next $21,840 of taxable income until it has eliminated the benefits of both their personal exemptions. Only then—at $171,090 of taxable income— would the 28% bracket start to apply again. If the couple had two children whom they claimed as dependents, the 33% bracket would apply over $43,680 ($10,920 × 4) of taxable income in excess of $149,250—or all the way up to $192,930— before the 28% bracket became effective again.

For a single person, the 33% bracket starts to eliminate the benefit of the personal exemption at taxable income of $89,560—the level of taxable income at which the benefit of the 15% bracket is eliminated. Therefore, for a single person with no dependents, the 33% bracket continues to apply until taxable income reaches $100,480 ($89,560 + $10,920), at which point the benefits of both the 15% bracket and the personal exemption are gone. Only then does the 28% bracket apply again.

Why has Congress used these complicated phase-out rules for the personal exemptions and the 15% bracket? Because it is a way of taxing income at the 33% bracket without actually saying so. You can call it a "phase-out of benefits," or you can call it a 33% rate. Congress, desiring to create the impression that the highest tax rate was 28%, called it a "phase-out of benefits." But you can now see that 28% is not the highest tax rate. For a married couple with no children, all their income between $71,900 and $171,090 is taxed at 33%—and more if they have children. For a single person with no dependents, all income between $43,150 and $100,480 is taxed at a 33% rate. Chances are that most higher income people will have most of their earnings taxed at 33%.

Under tax reform married couples who have taxable income in excess of $171,090 and whose children have income of their own may choose not to claim their children as dependents. The exemption for the child doesn't do them much good since its value is phased out by the 33% bracket. The exemption may save their child more tax than it saves them, but he can claim it on his tax return only if they don't claim an exemption for him on their return.

SUMMARY

Now that we have covered the personal exemptions, we have arrived at taxable income and are back to the tax rates which are applied against taxable income. We have nearly gone through a complete tax return, examining a majority of the changes that affect most people. It hasn't been an overwhelming amount of material to absorb. But while we have covered most of the changes that affect most people, we are not yet done. We still have some very important tax law changes to discuss—special-situation changes that affect special people, to be sure, but nonetheless of wide interest, like the new rules that affect your real estate investments, and tax shelters, and the family gift and trust rules. We will cover those changes and more, after we cover one last item—the tax credits, or at least what is left of them.

CHAPTER EIGHT

TAX CREDITS

Of all the ways of reducing your taxes, tax credits are the best—the equivalent of first prize or the brass ring. If you owe $3,000 in tax after completing your tax return, and are sitting there with a tax credit of $500, then you don't owe $3,000. You owe $2,500. Deductions are great—but they can't compare with tax credits. After tax reform, a $100 deduction means $15, $28, or $33 less in taxes, depending on your tax bracket. A $100 tax credit, on the other hand, is $100 in your pocket.

Even before the tax reform act, tax credits were scarce and hard to come by. After tax reform, it's all you can do to find some.

TAX CREDITS—YOU WIN SOME AND YOU LOSE SOME	
Popular tax credits repealed:	Contributions to political candidates Investment tax credit
Popular tax credits retained:	Child care credit Earned income credit Foreign tax credit Historic property renovation credit

WHAT'S GONE?

Political contributions credit repealed

One of the more popular tax credits before tax reform was the credit for contributions you made to candidates for public office. You got a credit equal to half the amount of your contribution, with a maximum credit of $100 for people who filed joint returns and $50 for single people. You would think that if any tax gimmick had survived tax reform, it would have been this one. But a majority of congressmen decided that they, too, had to suffer under tax reform, and the credit for political contributions was repealed.

Starting in 1987, there is no tax credit for political contributions. Note, however, that this credit was repealed right after an election year—which means that there's plenty of time to restore it before the next election!

Investment tax credit repealed

Before tax reform, the big credit was the investment tax credit. This was the one for rich people—it was a feature of many tax shelters—and for corporations. Under the investment tax credit rules you got a credit against your tax liability in the year in which you invested in certain property that you used in your business or in your investments—property such as automobiles, machinery, tractors, airplanes. The amount of the credit, with certain limitations, was 10% of what you paid for the property. If you bought a $10,000 machine for your business, you reduced your taxes by $1,000 for that year, just for buying some equipment that you probably needed anyway. It was one of the great tax incentives, but now it's gone. The investment tax credit was repealed. Property placed into service after December 31, 1985, does not qualify for the investment tax credit.

The tax reform act is not the first time that Congress has repealed the investment tax credit. This credit, which was first enacted in 1962, was suspended in 1966, reinstated in 1967, repealed in 1969, then re-enacted in 1971. The investment tax credit has resembled a revolving door in a department store because of its perceived impact on the economy. In 1962 it was felt that giving business an investment tax credit would stimulate modernization of American industry by encouraging corporations to invest in new plants and equipment. It worked, but by 1966 people were spending too much money on growth and inflation had taken over. So much for the investment tax credit. The credit came back in 1967 once inflation cooled, but then was repealed in 1969 when it became apparent that inflation would be around for a while. By 1971, unemployment had increased, and the credit was re-enacted to stimulate plant construction and job creation once again. The stated reason for repealing it under the tax reform act was the reduction in corporate tax rates. With lower taxes, Congress reasoned, there was no need for the investment tax credit: lower taxes would leave plenty of money for new investment. There is some truth to this rationale, but by 1986 another factor was at work. The investment tax credit was always supported by a strong lobby of manufacturing companies—companies that needed factories. By 1986, service companies played an equally important role in the American economy. Since businesses that provide services don't invest much in plants and equipment, they don't need the investment tax credit. With corporate lobbyists no longer lined up solidly behind the investment tax credit, the credit actually went out with little more than a whimper. It may be some time before you see an investment tax credit again. In fact, it may be forever.

Energy conservation credit expires

Many people have no doubt benefitted from the energy conservation credit. This credit, enacted in 1978 during the oil crisis, was available if you installed insulation, storm windows, more efficient furnaces, or other energy-conserving materials or machines in your home or place of business. But it was always set to expire after 1985, and in the 1986 tax reform act, Congress permitted it to do just that.

WHAT'S LEFT?

The child-care credit

The "child-care" or "dependent-care" credit was not affected by the tax reform act. This is the credit that you get when you pay someone to look after your children under the age of 15 while you work. This credit is also available if you have children 15 years old or over or other dependents (a parent or in-law) living in your house who cannot care for themselves. The credit equals 20% of the expenses that you incur for babysitters, nurses, or cleaning help, and it is higher if your adjusted gross income is less than $30,000, up to designated maximums.

Other credits

Several more credits, for special people, survived tax reform. Low-income people with children still get the "earned income credit," and elderly people with low incomes also receive a special credit. People who pay taxes to foreign countries still get the "foreign tax credit."

Another credit that survived tax reform is for people who renovate historic property. We'll look at this credit in Chapter 12.

CHAPTER NINE

CAPITAL GAINS

The bad news is that the 1986 tax reform act repealed the special tax treatment for capital gains. The worse news is that tax reform did *not* repeal the very complicated rules that surround capital gains.

The capital gains rules have always been among the most baffling of the tax laws. It was often said that you paid tax on only 40% of your capital gains, but that was never quite true. Before tax reform, you paid tax on only 40% of your "net long-term capital gains." The hard part of capital gains has always been to figure out just what your "net long-term capital gains" were. Schedule D of Form 1040—or at least the first 25 lines of it—is the best evidence of how difficult that can be. Even after tax reform, the complexity remains. You will still have to complete Schedule D if you have capital gains because the new tax act did not simplify the capital gains rules. It simply raised the amount of tax that you pay on your capital gains.

NETTING CAPITAL GAINS

When you buy and sell stocks and bonds, or artwork, gold, houses, or buildings, you can have several different kinds of capital transactions. It all depends on how long you've held the property that you sell and on whether you sell at a gain or a loss. For example, if you buy stock and hold it for more than six months, then sell it at a profit, your profit is called a "long-term capital gain." If after six months, you sell that stock at a loss, then you have a "long-term capital loss."

The result changes if you hold that stock for *six months or less*. Then, any profits are "short-term capital gains." And any losses that you incur are "short-term capital losses." These rules apply even after tax reform.

After you have determined the term and the amount of your gain or loss for each property sold during the year, you balance all these gains and losses together. First, you balance your long-term transactions: the long-term capital gains against any long-term capital losses—you reduce your long-term gains by your long-term losses. That gives you either an overall gain or an overall loss (depending on how well you invested) for your long-term capital transactions. Next, you balance your short-term capital transactions. You offset short-term gains with short-term losses, and you arrive at an overall gain or loss for your short-term transactions.

You did this balancing before tax reform, and you still do it under the new tax act.

FIGURING CAPITAL GAINS

Having determined your overall gains or losses for long-term transactions, and your overall gains or losses for short-term transactions, now you try to balance the long-term results against the short-term results. If you have an overall long-term gain and an overall short-term loss, for example, you can balance that. So you offset your overall long-term gain by your overall short-term loss. Let us suppose that you sell four capital assets in a certain year with the following results.

Asset #1	$2000 long-term gain	Asset #3	$500 short-term gain
Asset #2	1000 long-term loss	Asset #4	800 short-term loss
Net	$1000 long-term gain	Net	$300 short-term loss

Result: a *net long-term capital gain* for the year of $700. Before tax reform, you took 60% of that gain, or $420, and you put it in your pocket. That $420 was tax-free money unless you were subject to a beast called the "alternative minimum tax" (see Chapter 13). The remaining 40%, or $280, was added to the rest of your income and taxed at the regular rates that applied before tax reform—12%, 14%, or up to 50%, depending on your tax bracket.

Under tax reform, you can no longer put the $420 in your pocket. Instead, your entire net long-term capital gain of $700 is added to your other income and taxed at whatever tax bracket you are in—15%, 28%, or 33% once tax reform is fully phased in. (However, the maximum rate on capital gains for 1987 is 28%.) *This loss of your ability to put 60% of your net long-term capital gain in your pocket, with one exception, is the only substantive change in the capital gains rules made by the tax reform act.* It is effective for capital assets sold after December 31, 1986.

After tax reform, any kind of a gain or loss, besides a net long-term capital gain, is taxed just as it was before tax reform with that one additional exception that we will get to. Let's return to our example where we had a $1,000 long-term gain and a $300 short-term loss. But suppose that the term of our gains and losses had been reversed, so that our $1,000 gain was short-term, and our $300 loss was long-term. We can balance that to arrive at a $700 net *short-term* capital gain. Prior to tax reform, a net short-term capital gain was simply added to your other income and taxed at the regular rates. No part of a short-term gain ever went into your pocket. The same is true under the tax reform act. The entire net short-term gain is added to your other income.

One final example on gains. Suppose we'd

had good luck with both our long-term and short-term investments and, instead of having a $300 short-term loss, we'd had a $300 short-term gain in addition to our $1,000 long-term gain. You can't balance a gain with a gain. Before and after tax reform, the $300 short-term gain is included in your other income and taxed at the regular rates. And, after tax reform, the entire long-term gain is also added to your other income and taxed at the regular rates.

Why, you might ask, if all your short-term gains *and* long-term gains are now added to your other income, why must you account for them separately? The answer to this question lies in the treatment of capital losses.

CAPITAL LOSSES

Suppose, in our example, our gains and losses were reversed, so that we had an overall $1,000 long-term *loss* and an overall $300 short-term *gain*. We can balance that, and we get a "net long-term capital loss" of $700. Before tax reform, you got a deduction for that loss: every $2 of net long-term capital loss could be used to reduce $1 of your salary, dividends and other income. Therefore, you used your $700 long-term loss to produce a $350 deduction. After tax reform, however, long-term capital losses can be deducted dollar for dollar against your other income. This is the other major change in the capital gains rules that we referred to earlier.

Before tax reform, if our $700 net loss, instead of being *long-term*, had been a *short-term* capital loss, we got a deduction for that, too. But instead of having to use $2 of loss to offset $1 of income (as with long-term losses), net short-term capital losses could just reduce other income dollar for dollar. Therefore, a $700 net short-term loss produced a full $700 deduction. After tax reform, no change. Tax reform changed only the treatment of net *long-term* capital *gains* and the $2 for $1 rule of long-term capital losses.

Finally, if our investments were disastrous during the year, and we had both long-term and short-term losses, we first claimed the short-term losses as a deduction, dollar for dollar, and then claimed the long-term losses as a deduction, two dollars for one dollar. This applies both before and after tax reform, except that long-term losses are now deductible dollar for dollar.

Once again, why must we account for all these transactions separately? There is no longer any real need to account for short-term and long-term transactions separately because, after tax reform, there is no difference in the tax results they produce. Nonetheless, Congress has left the long-term and short-term rules in the tax code in case it decides to reinstate the tax break for long-term gains. Gains and losses in general, on the other hand, whether long-term or short-term, must be accounted for separately because before and after tax reform there is a limitation on the amount of deductions that can be generated by capital losses in any one year. That limitation is $3,000. If you have a capital loss of $4,000, you can use only $3,000 of it in any one year as a deduction from other income. Before and after tax reform.

What happens to the $1,000 in capital losses that you can't use? They are *carried over* to the next year. You store your unused capital losses away and bring them out in the next year to balance them against any capital gains that you might have that year. An unused capital loss is called a "capital loss carryover" and is applied against any capital gains you might have in the following year, or it can be used to generate an additional $3,000 deduction in the following year. If you don't use up that capital loss in the following year, you can store it away until the next year—and you keep carrying it over until you do use it.

Suppose that in one year you had $1,000 of unused short-term or long-term capital loss, and in the next year, after doing your balancing act, you had a $2,000 net long-term capital gain. Then you bring out your $1,000 capital loss carryover, and you balance it against the $2,000 long-term gain. Result: instead of paying tax on $2,000 in gain in the next year, you pay tax on only $1,000 in gain. It has always been important to keep track of your capital loss carryovers, but after tax reform it is even more important. Since those net long-term capital gains, which used to be 60% tax free, are fully taxable under tax reform, you now want to be sure to carry forward any unused capital losses to offset against any capital gains that you realize in the future.

Congress could have eliminated the need for this separate accounting and balancing—and with it most of the complexity of capital gains—simply by eliminating the $3,000 limit on deductions for capital losses. Before tax reform, the fact that only a portion of your capital gains was taxed was at least partial justification for permitting you to deduct only a portion of your losses. What was fair for gains was fair for losses. Now that tax reform has made all your capital gains taxable, why not permit a deduction for all your losses? That would have been major simplification. But it also would have cost the government a great deal of revenue. Therefore, the good part of capital gains is gone, and the limitations on deducting losses, with all the complexity of figuring capital gains, remain.

SELLING YOUR HOME

Tax reform did not have any special effect on the tax consequences of selling your home. However, your home is a capital asset and, unless you roll over the gain on a sale, you have a capital gain when you sell it. This is a long-term capital gain if you've owned your home more than six months. Before tax reform, you could put 60% of that gain in your pocket. After tax reform, the entire gain is subject to tax.

The 1986 tax reform act does not affect the rollover rules for home sales. If, within two years (before or after) the sale of your home, you buy a new home for which you pay more than you sold your old home for, the gain from the sale of the old home still goes untaxed. Instead of paying tax on that gain, you reduce the tax cost of your new home by the amount of the gain. That gain will eventually be taxed when you sell the new home without buying another new home. If that gain is ever taxed, under tax reform all of it will be taxed—rather than only 40% of it—but as long as you keep rolling it over there is no tax.

People aged 55 or older who sell their homes can still exclude $125,000 of the gain that they realize on the sale. Whatever gain remains, however, is then fully taxed under tax reform (unless the gain is rolled over into a new home).

The new tax act did not affect the computation of gain on the sale of your home. It did not affect the rollover rules. It did not affect the $125,000 exclusion rule. Tax reform merely says that, once you have determined the amount of your net long-term capital gain and once you have determined that the gain is presently subject to tax, then all of it is taxed, not just 40% as under the prior law.

CHAPTER TEN

HOME OFFICE DEDUCTIONS AND HOBBY LOSSES

I f you use part of your home in your trade or business, chances are you claim a "home-office deduction." You write off the portion of the expenses of maintaining your home—repairs, fuel, electricity, insurance—that are allocable to the portion of your home that you use for business. You can even depreciate the portion of your home used for business. For example, if you use one room of an eight-room house for your business, you deduct one-eighth of the expenses of maintaining your home and claim a depreciation deduction with respect to one-eighth of the cost of your home. These deductions are not allowed if you use your home solely as your residence. As a general rule, in order to claim these expenses, you must use a portion of your home as the "principal place" of your trade or business, or at least as a place where you meet customers or clients or patients. Also, you must use that portion of your home exclusively for business purposes—no family matters can take place in there—and on a regular basis.

Assuming that what you do in your home makes you eligible for the home-office deduction, there are limitations on the amount of home-related expenses that you can claim. One of these limitations is related to how much money you make from the business carried on in your home. Prior to tax reform, the law said that your home office deductions could not exceed the amount of gross income you derived from the business. This law seemed simple enough. If you were a part-time writer, for example, and you worked at home and made $10,000 during the year, your home-office deductions—the portion of the insurance, utilities, and rent or depreciation allocable to the part of your home used for business—could not exceed $10,000. At least, that was what the law appeared to say.

The IRS, however, said that the law did *not* say that. What the law said, according to the IRS, was that the home-office deduction could not exceed the *net* income from your business. First you reduced your gross income from the business by your business expenses—and what remained was the limit on your home-office deduction. Take our writer making $10,000 per year; if he spent $5,000 on supplies and on travel and transportation—non-home-office expenses —then the income he derived from his business was $5,000, not $10,000, the IRS said, and his maximum home-office deduction was $5,000.

Is *that* what the law said? No, the Tax Court said, that wasn't what the law said. What the law said was just what it said: the home-office deduction was limited to the *gross* income derived from the business. Gross income meant gross income—not gross income reduced by other business expenses besides the home-office deduction. For our writer, the limit was $10,000, according to the Tax Court.

Just what did this law say? According to the Congress, it said what the IRS said it said. Or if it hasn't said that in the past, that's what it now says after tax reform. Starting in 1987, home-office deductions are limited to the gross income derived from the business carried on in your home less the non-home-office expenses that you claim in connection with that business. For our writer, $5,000 is the limit on his home-office deductions.

FIGURING THE HOME-OFFICE DEDUCTION

Gross income from business in your home:	$10,000
Business expenses (supplies, travel, etc.):	− 5,000
Net income from business in your home:	5,000
Maximum limit on home-office tax deduction:	5,000

Congress often takes advantage of major tax legislation to clear up these little misunderstandings—particularly misunderstandings that cost the government money!

HOBBY LOSSES

If you have a little business on the side, often the question arises as to whether you really intend to make any money from this business—that is, whether you have a "profit motive" in the way you conduct your business. The question of profit motive is most significant when your side business consists of something you like to do anyway as a hobby.

For example, suppose your hobby is carpentry and you like to build things in your basement on the weekends. You buy several fancy tools and machines, and spend a good deal of money on lumber, nails, and various finishings. Every now and then a neighbor visits your workshop, sees a table or desk that you built, and buys it. Before you know it, you're in the carpentry business. You include as income the money that your neighbor pays you, and you deduct all the money you spend on raw materials as well as the depreciation of your tools and machines. You also start to claim a home-office deduction for the allocable cost of your basement. Since you don't try very hard to sell anything that you build, it turns out that every year your carpentry "business" suffers losses, which you deduct from your salary or other income.

The tax law calls this kind of loss a "hobby loss" and puts restrictions on claiming it. If your carpentry work generates some income but you don't really try to make it a profitable business— that is, you lack a "profit motive"—under the law you can claim deductions from your hobby up to the amount of the income that you make from the hobby, but no more. The expenses of your hobby can reduce the income that your hobby produces, but they can't be used to offset income from other sources, such as your salary.

Under the "hobby loss" rule, the important question becomes: when do you have a profit motive? How does the government tell when you intend to make money from your carpentry and when you are just having a good time and don't care if you make money? The IRS has a nine-part objective test for determining whether you have a profit motive; but this nine-part test often generates litigation, at great cost to both you and the IRS. In an attempt to prevent litigation over profit motive, the IRS has come up with an alternative test. Before tax reform, this alternative test was called the "two-out-of-five" rule. If you actually made a profit from your carpentry in two out of every five years, then a presumption arose that you had a profit motive and, unless the IRS could prove otherwise, all the expenses of your carpentry work were deductible. If you did not make a profit in at least two of every five years, a presumption arose that

PLAYING YOUR HOBBY LOSS	
Old tax law:	You must make a profit from your side business or hobby in *two* out of every five years in order to deduct your business losses.
New tax law:	You must make a profit from your side business or hobby in *three* out of every five years in order to deduct your business losses.
Period:	Five years starting when you first show a profit; to rely on the presumption in 1987, you must meet the three out of five rule by then.

you did not have a profit motive and, unless you could prove otherwise, your hobby losses were disallowed.

Under the 1986 tax reform act, the "two-out-of-five" rule has become a "three-out-of-five" rule. Starting in 1987, you must show a profit in three of every five years if you want a presumption to arise that you have a profit motive and are entitled to deduct all the expenses of your side business. While this change is effective as of 1987, if you have had a side business since 1983, you may be in for a surprise. The law says that if you want to rely on the presumption to deduct a loss from a side business in 1987, then by 1987 it must be possible for you to satisfy the "three-out-of-five" rule. If you had your business in 1983, 1984, and 1985, and you lost money on it in 1985, you cannot rely on the presumption to claim a loss from it in 1987 because it will be impossible to satisfy the "three-out-of-five" rule.

At this point you may think that Congress has changed the rules in the middle of the game. Your thinking is correct!

CHAPTER ELEVEN

DEPRECIATION

WHAT IS DEPRECIATION?

Depreciation is a deduction that you get because you own property which decreases in value. The strange thing about depreciation, though, is that your property doesn't really have to decrease in value. It just has to decrease in value for purposes of the tax laws. And under the tax laws, everything decreases in value—even if it actually increases in value!

If you bought a house for $100,000 and sold it the next year, somebody would probably pay you up to $110,000 for it. That is what it would be worth. If you sold it after two years, someone might pay you up to $121,000 for it. In real life, residential property often increases in value at rates as high as 10 percent per year—and even higher in some locations.

In the fantasy world of the tax laws, however, property decreases in value. After all, property gets older every year. In a house the plaster starts to crack, the roof leaks, and the wood rots around the windows. The property just wastes away. It may well be worth more every year in dollars, but it is wasting away just the same. Under the tax law, you get a deduction for that. It's called a depreciation deduction.

You can take a depreciation deduction for all tangible business or investment property except land. Houses, buildings, automobiles, machines, airplanes—all tangible business property used in a business or investment, except land, is depreciable. The fact is, a great deal of business property does decrease in value because a great deal of business property is machinery. But some business property is real estate, and in the real world that rarely decreases in value. Nonetheless, the tax code says it decreases in value, so you still get a depreciation deduction.

STRAIGHT-LINE DEPRECIATION AND USEFUL LIVES

What is the amount of the depreciation deduction? The amount of the depreciation deduction is the amount by which your property is said to decrease in value each year. The kind of property which individuals own is often said to decrease in value evenly— that is, by the same amount each year for a number of years. That amount depends on your "basis" in the property—which is usually what you paid for it—and on how long you can expect it to be useful. If you paid $1,000 for it and you expect to be able to use it for five years and then throw it away, it decreases in value $200 each year. That is your yearly depreciation deduction.

Under the tax laws, when property is said to decrease in value evenly over its useful life, we call that "straight-line depreciation." If you plotted the decrease in value of your property on a graph, the value would fall in a straight line. Sometimes property is said to decrease in value even faster, which we call "accelerated depreciation"—a subject to which we will return.

How do you know how long you can expect your property to be useful? Determining a useful life acceptable both to you and to the IRS was once one of the more problematic areas of the tax law. Taxpayers usually wanted to assign a shorter useful life to property so that they could claim more depreciation in the early years of ownership. The IRS would assign a longer useful life—forcing the taxpayer to claim depreciation in smaller amounts over a longer period of time. A great deal of effort and money was spent by taxpayers, the IRS, and tax court judges in trying to agree on accurate useful lives for all the different kinds of property used by business taxpayers.

In 1981, Congress put an end to the "useful life" problem for most kinds of property. It enacted legislation that assigned useful lives to classes of property for the purpose of computing depreciation. The legislation in effect said: "Taxpayers and the IRS will no longer argue about the useful life of business property. Instead, the property's useful life shall be as follows."

What followed were several classes of property. Different kinds of property were assigned to each class. And each class was given its own useful life. For example, cars were assigned to a "3-year" class of property and were to be depreciated, therefore, over 3 years. There would be no more arguments over the useful life of a car. Most other equipment was in a 5-year class of property and was to be depreciated over 5 years. Real estate was placed in a 15-year class, and in subsequent tax acts the period for depreciating real estate was increased to 19 years.

Under tax reform, the classes are changed. Cars are no longer in the 3-year class but now are in the 5-year class and are to be depreciated over 5 years. Most business equipment, instead of being only in the 5-year class, is now divided between the 5-year class and a new 7-year class. The exact class which business equipment is in depends on something called its "Asset Depreciation Range Midpoint Life." These midpoint lives are assigned to property by the IRS, and you will have to ask your tax advisor which class—5 years or 7 years—a particular piece of equipment is in. Residential real estate is now in a 27.5-year class, and commercial property—all real property that is not residential property—is now in a 31.5-year class.

To calculate straight-line depreciation after tax reform, you determine which new class your property falls in and then divide the cost of the property by the number of years which describes that class—3 or 5 or 7, and so on up to 31.5 years for commercial real estate.

ACCELERATED DEPRECIATION

When you depreciate property under an accelerated method of depreciation, you don't depreciate it evenly over its designated life. You take more depreciation in the earlier years that you own the property and less depreciation in the later years. Accelerated depreciation is allowed in recognition of the fact that property declines faster in value early in its economic life. It also helps you to recover your investment in property quickly, enabling you to invest in more property.

Until 1981 there were many methods of accelerated depreciation. The most advantageous was the "double declining balance" method of depreciation—also called the "200 percent" method. Under this method, your depreciation deduction in the first year that you owned the property was double what it would be under the straight-line method, but in the following years it steadily decreased until eventually it became less than the annual depreciation you would claim under the straight-line method. Under tax reform, it is once again important to understand this 200% method of accelerated depreciation, so here is how it worked.

In the first year, you figured out what your depreciation deduction would be under the straight-line method and then doubled it; that was your depreciation deduction for the first year. For a $35,000 machine with a useful life of seven years, for example, the depreciation deduction under the straight-line method would be $5,000 each year. Under the 200% method, in the first year the depreciation deduction would be $10,000. But from there the depreciation you claimed each year under this method started to decline. The reason for this decline was that, when you used the 200% method, each year you had to compute your depreciation deduction all over again and, before you did, you had to reduce your basis in the property by the amount of the deduction which you had claimed the year before. So in the second year that you owned your $35,000 machine, your basis for computing the depreciation deduction was only $25,000 ($35,000 original cost less $10,000 of depreciation claimed in the first year). You figured out what straight-line depreciation would be with that basis ($25,000 ÷ 7, or $3,571.50) and then you doubled it ($7,143). In the second year, your depreciation deduction under the 200% method was $7,143—and so on for the following years. Your depreciation deductions over four years for a $35,000 machine with a useful life of seven years, under the 200% method, is shown in the accompanying box.

Accelerated depreciation did not get you more total depreciation, it just got you more depreciation sooner. In fact, overall, you got less depreciation under this method. In later years, the amount of the annual depreciation deduction fell below the amount available under the straight-line method. You can see in the example below that, by the fourth year, the deductible depreciation was less than it would be under the straight-line method—$3,644 rather than $5,000. If you continued the calculations through seven years, you would see that you actually lost about $3,300 in depreciation overall. But you did not have to lose that $3,300 in depreciation. Once your deductible depreciation fell below what it would be under the straight-line method, the IRS permitted you to return to the straight-line method for the remainder of the property's useful life in order to fully depreciate it. Depreciation was then calculated on the property's reduced basis at the time, less salvage value.

FIGURING ACCELERATED DEPRECIATION	
Cost	$35,000
First-year deduction	
$35,000 ÷ 7 × 2	10,000
New basis	$25,000
Second-year depreciation	
$25,000 ÷ 7 × 2	7,143
New basis	$17,857
Third-year depreciation	
$17,857 ÷ 7 × 2	5,102
New basis	$12,755
Fourth-year depreciation	
$12,755 ÷ 7 × 2	3,644
And so on, through seven years.	

Before 1981, another popular method of calculating accelerated depreciation was the "150 percent method"—identical to the "200 percent method" except that you started by claiming one and one-half times as much depreciation—rather than twice as much—as would have been claimed under the straight-line method.

In 1981, most of the different methods of accelerated depreciation—and, more important, the complicated calculations associated with them—were eliminated. In their place, Congress prescribed a relatively simple method of depreciation which gave you approximately the same result as under the various old methods of accelerated depreciation.

We saw earlier that in 1981 Congress said that, for purposes of determining the useful life of property, most property was to be divided into three categories; automobiles in one category; all other tangible personal property in the second; and most real estate in the third. Congress also stated that, for people who wished to use accelerated methods of depreciation, designated percentages called "recovery rates" were to be used, depending on the class of property being depreciated. For automobiles and other property in the three-year class, accelerated depreciation was calculated as follows:

In the first year that you owned the property, your depreciation deduction was 25 percent of the cost of the property. Period—there were no more complicated calculations. You just multiplied your basis in the property by 25%, and you had your accelerated depreciation deduction for the year. In the second year of ownership, your accelerated depreciation was 38 percent of cost, and in the third year, 37 percent of cost. That was how you calculated accelerated depreciation for "three-year property." It was that simple. There were other recovery rates for five-year property and for real estate which made the calculation of accelerated depreciation for these classes of property equally simple.

You will never guess what Congress has done under tax reform. It has repealed the "recovery rate" procedure for calculating accelerated depreciation and resurrected the old 200% and 150% methods that were used prior to 1981. After tax reform, we are back to the complex calculations again—figure out straight-line depreciation, double it, reduce the cost, and start all over again. The old law is the new law!

Under tax reform, however, there is one difference from the pre-1981 rules. Prior to 1981, you could choose your method of accelerated depreciation. You could use the 200% method, or the 150% method, or a 125% method, or other more esoteric methods. With the tax reform act of 1986, your choice is narrowed. For three-year, five-year, seven-year, and ten-year property, you must use either the 200% method or the straight-line method of depreciation. (For special assets, however, such as movie films, special methods of depreciation are still used.) For all other property except real estate, you must use either the 150% method or the straight-line method. And for real estate, only the straight-line method may be used.

In summary, after tax reform you still must look to classes of property to determine useful life. The classes have been changed, and new classes have been added, but all depreciable property still fits into one of these classes. However, after you figure out which class your property is in, then you calculate depreciation under the pre-1981 rules, using the 200% method or straight-line depreciation for three-year, five-year, and seven-year property, and the 150% method or straight-line depreciation for all other property except real estate. Real estate must be depreciated under the straight-line method.

The new depreciation rules apply to property "placed in service" after December 31, 1986. Property is placed in service when you first start to use it in your trade or business. Therefore, if you started to use a new machine in your business (or invested in real estate) in 1986, you will continue to depreciate that property under the rules in effect since 1981. The new rules of tax reform apply only to property placed in service after 1986.

Expensing depreciable property

When you buy depreciable property other than real estate to use in your business (not in an investment) you are permitted to deduct a portion of the cost of that property in the year that you first use it. Before tax reform, the maximum amount of this first-year deduction in any year was $5,000. Under tax reform, starting with property placed in service after 1986, the maximum deduction is $10,000 per year. However, this deduction is now available only for businesses that don't spend large sums of money on depreciable property in any one year. If you spend more than $200,000 on depreciable business property (not counting real estate) in any one year, the allowable amount of this deduction is reduced by $1 for each dollar by which your spending exceeds $200,000. Once you spend $210,000, the deduction is phased out altogether. Also, under tax reform, the amount of this deduction cannot exceed your taxable income from the business. If your first-year deduction is $8,000 but your taxable income from the business is only $5,000, only $5,000 of that first-year deduction can be claimed. Whatever portion is not claimed under this limitation can be carried forward and used in a later year when your taxable income allows for it. (In determining taxable income from your business in order to decide whether you can claim all or a portion of the first-year deduction, you claim all your other business expenses but you don't claim the first-year deduction.)

CHAPTER TWELVE

REAL ESTATE

THE AT-RISK RULE

Since 1976, Congress' main weapon against abusive tax shelters has been the so-called "at risk" rule. Real estate tax shelters, however, have always received special treatment from Congress, and before the tax reform act of 1986 they were not subject to the at-risk rule at all. After tax reform, all investments in real estate are subject to the at-risk rule, but most of these investments, as we will see, will not be affected.

Under the at-risk rule, the greatest amount of tax loss which you can claim on your investments in any year is the amount of money which you have "at risk." If an investment throws off a tax loss of $20,000 in a particular year but you only have $10,000 at risk in the investment, then you can claim only $10,000 of that $20,000 loss. For example, suppose you decided to purchase a computer which you intended to rent out to other people at a cost of $100,000. Suppose also that the computer manufacturing company was willing to finance your purchase of this computer. If you put $10,000 cash down you could pay for this computer over 5 years, perhaps using rental income to help pay for it. The manufacturer, in effect, has loaned you $90,000. Suppose, in addition, that the computer manufacturing company agreed not to hold you personally responsible for repaying this loan. If you failed to repay the loan, the company agreed to take back the computer and let you off the hook.

When you make an arrangement like that, the $90,000 loan from the manufacturer is called a "nonrecourse" loan. It's a loan secured by property, and if you don't pay it back, all you lose is the property which secures it. You are not personally responsible for paying the loan back.

Under the at-risk rule, you are not "at risk" for that $90,000 loan. In your purchase of the computer, you are at risk only for the $10,000 cash that you put down. Had that $90,000 loan been a "recourse" loan—a loan that you were personally obligated to repay—then you would have been at risk for the full amount of the loan. Recourse loans put you at risk, nonrecourse loans don't. If your computer rental business threw off a $20,000 loss, under the at-risk rule only $10,000 of that loss could be claimed.

Whether or not you could make such an arrangement with a computer manufacturer, commercial real estate deals typically involve nonrecourse loans. When you buy commercial real property, you usually make a small cash downpayment and give a large "nonrecourse" note.

At first, the at-risk rule applied only to investments in a few kinds of property which were often used in tax shelters, such as oil and gas properties and equipment. Then, in 1978, the at-risk rule was made applicable to investments in all property *except real estate*. Now, with tax reform, all real estate investments are also subject to the at-risk rule. However, whether an investment in real estate will be affected by the at-risk rule depends on how you finance it.

It is easy to understand the new at-risk rule for

MAKING AT-RISK REAL ESTATE LOANS MORE RISKY

Before tax reform, the at-risk rule did not apply to real estate. After tax reform, real estate investments are subject to the at-risk rule. *But*, most bank-financed real estate transactions will not be affected by the at-risk rule because the rule is targeted at seller-financed transactions used by tax shelter promoters.

93

real estate if you understand the abuse that Congress was attacking by enacting it. Real estate is depreciable property, and the more you pay for the property, the higher your depreciation deductions. If you buy real property principally with a nonrecourse loan, you are less concerned about what you pay for it, since you don't have to repay the loan personally. Therefore, some real estate entrepreneurs, or tax-shelter promoters, would agree to buy real estate at an inflated purchase price, paying for most of that inflated price with nonrecourse loans. By paying an artificially high price, they obtained greater depreciation deductions; by using nonrecourse loans, they did not increase their risk.

Entrepreneurs and tax shelter promoters often obtained nonrecourse loans from the seller of the property, who was delighted to receive an inflated purchase price—often the seller was another tax shelter promoter. These transactions were "seller-financed" and banks were not involved. However, when you borrow money from a bank to buy real estate, the bank is unlikely to make a loan for more than the property is truly worth. Banks don't lend money to pay inflated purchase prices. Therefore, as a general rule, under tax reform if you borrow money from a bank to buy real estate, *you will be considered at-risk* for the loan even if it is nonrecourse.

Borrowing from other people who are "actively and regularly engaged in the business of lending money" will also put you at risk even if the borrowing is nonrecourse. You can finance a real estate purchase with a nonrecourse loan from a savings and loan institution, a credit union, an insurance company, a pension trust, or other regular money-lender, but you will be considered at risk for the full amount of the loan even though it is a nonrecourse loan. Therefore, even though the at-risk rule applies to all real estate investments, it doesn't have any effect on bank-financed investments because bank financing is deemed to be money at-risk.

The at-risk rule for real estate comes into play under tax reform only when you borrow money on a nonrecourse basis from someone other than a bank. Under the tax reform law, you are not at risk on a nonrecourse loan in a real estate acquisition if you borrow money from someone not in the business of lending money. And, perhaps most important, you are not at risk if the person you borrow from is the same person who is selling the property. Even if the seller is a bank or other regular money-lender, you are not at risk on a nonrecourse loan if the lender is selling you the property. Congress obviously thought that a bank might be more willing to take back an inflated nonrecourse note if it was also the seller. Therefore, nonrecourse seller-financing never gives you at-risk status.

The new at-risk rule for real estate will not affect the great majority of commercial real estate transactions involving third-party financing. The rule is aimed at the tax shelter promoters who arrange for sales of real estate among themselves and their investors at inflated purchase prices. And remember, the at-risk rule applies only if there is a *nonrecourse* loan. If a loan holds you personally responsible for repayment, it is a recourse loan and you are fully at risk for the amount of the loan. Even if the seller finances your purchase of the property, you are at risk if you give him a recourse note. The at-risk rules, and the historic property renovation rules discussed below, apply generally to property placed in service after December 31, 1986.

HISTORIC REAL PROPERTY

In the tax reform act, Congress also made changes in the rules that affect investments in special kinds of real estate. One of these changes involves historic property.

Since 1976, Congress has provided tax incentives to people who renovate historic property. After tax reform, these incentives still exist, but they have been curtailed.

The incentive for rehabilitating historic property is a tax credit. When we talked about tax credits in Chapter 8, we said that some special credits had survived tax reform. The historic property rehabilitation credit is one of them.

If you spend money fixing up historic property, you get a tax credit—not a deduction, but a credit—equal to a percentage of the money you spend. There are some ground rules to qualify for this credit. First, the property that you fix up has to be "historic" property. Historic property is property that is listed in the *National Register of Historic Landmarks,* a list of properties designated as historic by the Department of the Interior. Property that is located in an area that has been certified by your state as an historic district—and that bears some relevance to the historic character of the area—is also historic property for purposes of this tax credit.

Second, the property has to be rehabilitated in accordance with federal historic property guidelines. You must preserve the historic value of the property and obtain a certification from the Interior Department that you have done so in order to qualify for this credit.

Third, after the renovation you must use the property as your place of business or rent it out to someone else. There is no tax credit for rehabilitating an historic property that you live in.

CHANGES IN THE TAX CREDIT
FOR REHABILITATING PROPERTY

HISTORIC PROPERTY	% OF REHABILITATION COST
Tax credit before tax reform	25%
Tax credit after tax reform	20%
OLD BUILDINGS	
Tax credit before tax reform	15% for buildings 30 years old or older 20% for buildings 40 years old or older
Tax credit after tax reform	10% for buildings placed in service before 1936

If you meet these three criteria (and others discussed below), your renovation qualifies for the tax credit. Before the tax reform act, the credit was 25% of the money you spent on renovation. After tax reform, it is 20% of the renovation expenditures.

To qualify for this credit before tax reform, in renovating historic property you had to preserve a certain percentage of the property's original structure. You could satisfy this "original structure" requirement in either of two ways: you could retain 75% of the property's external walls; or you could retain 75% of the property's internal structural framework, 50% of its external walls as external walls, and 75% of its external walls as external or internal walls. Under tax reform, these tests no longer apply. A renovation qualifies for the credit as long as it is certified by the Interior Department.

One final change in the historic property rules. Even though you claim a tax credit for your rehabilitation expenditures, you are still entitled to depreciate the property. Your depreciation is based on what the property cost you—the purchase price plus rehabilitation costs. Before tax reform, in calculating depreciation you had to reduce your cost of the property by one-half the amount of the credit that you claimed. So if you paid $50,000 for the property and spent $100,000 in renovating it, you claimed a credit of $25,000 (25% of $100,000). In calculating depreciation, you reduced the total cost of the property ($150,000) by $12,500 (one-half of $25,000). But under the new tax act, you must reduce your cost by the *full* amount of the credit. Thus the credit for the same renovation would be $20,000 (20% of $100,000), and your cost for purposes of computing depreciation would be reduced by the whole $20,000 credit that you claimed.

OLD BUILDINGS

Before tax reform, you also benefitted from a tax credit if you fixed up buildings that were just plain old, even though they were not historic. The amount of the credit depended on how old the building was; for buildings at least 30 years old, the credit was 15% of the renovation expenditures; for buildings at least 40 years old, the credit was 20% of the renovation costs. After tax reform, there is only one credit for old buildings—it is 10% of the rehabilitation costs, and it applies to nonhistoric buildings placed in service before 1936. As with historic property, you cannot reside in the property.

In calculating depreciation for renovated old buildings, you must reduce the cost of the property by the full amount of the tax credit that you claim. In addition, for nonhistoric old buildings, you must still meet the "original structure" requirement that once applied to historic buildings. However, the first test, which required only that 75% of the property's external walls be retained, has been repealed. The renovation of an old building must meet the alternative "original structure" test to qualify for the credit.

CHAPTER THIRTEEN

TAX SHELTERS: CONGRESS DROPS THE BOMB

Tax shelters have been under attack by Congress since 1976, when the at-risk rule was first enacted. Since then, Congress has made a number of attempts to curtail the use of tax shelters. It has expanded the at-risk rule; it has imposed penalties on the people who promote tax shelters; it has required that tax shelters be registered with the IRS. The Congress has imposed penalties on people whose tax shelter deductions are disallowed and has required these people to pay interest on tax underpayments at higher rates than other people. It has even tried to make lawyers and accountants accountable for the tax advice they give regarding tax shelters—and more.

Each of these attempts at curbing tax shelters was directed at a specific problem which seemed to facilitate the use of tax shelters. Taken altogether, however, these efforts did not have the impact that Congress had hoped for. In 1986, tax shelters still thrived. Therefore, in the tax reform act, Congress dropped THE BOMB. The Bomb has a name; it is called the "passive loss rule." The passive loss rule not only obliterates tax shelters; its fallout affects many perfectly legitimate investments as well.

PASSIVE LOSSES DISALLOWED

Under tax reform, losses from a "passive trade or business activity" may be used only to offset income from another passive trade or business activity. So-called "passive losses" may not be deducted against income from other sources, such as salary, dividends, interest, or capital gains.

The impact of this passive loss rule obviously

depends on the definition of "passive trade or business activity." In fact, the definition is a broad one. For all activities except those involving real estate and oil and gas, an activity is a passive one if (1) it involves the conduct of a trade or business and (2) you do not "materially participate" in that trade or business. (We will get to real estate and oil and gas activities shortly.)

DON'T BE PASSIVE ABOUT
THE PASSIVE LOSS RULE

A passive trade or business activity is one in which you don't "materially participate" in its day-to-day operations. The "passive loss rule" provides that a loss from a passive business activity can be offset only by income from that or another passive activity. But there are some exceptions to the passive loss rule.

A tax shelter partnership is an obvious "passive trade or business activity" (which we shall now call simply a "passive activity"). In a tax shelter partnership, the partnership itself carries on a trade or business. It may lease equipment, pursue research and development, publish a newsletter, mine for gold or coal, or conduct any one of a number of businesses that tax shelter partnerships have historically engaged in. But in a tax shelter partnership you are a limited partner; you do not participate at all in the day-to-day operations of this business—you are not even permitted to participate. Since the partnership is conducting a business, and since you do not materially participate in that business, your interest in the partnership is a passive activity. Any losses which are generated by the partnership may not be deducted by you except against income generated by the partnership in a later year or by another passive activity. If you are a limited partner in another partnership which produces income for you, you can reduce that income by the losses of your loss partnership. But those losses cannot be deducted against any other kind of income.

Many tax shelters are structured through an S corporation instead of a partnership. Clearly, an S corporation carrying on a business in which you do not materially participate is also a "passive activity" with respect to you, and the same limitation on the deduction of losses applies.

So much for activities which are clearly tax shelters. The passive loss rule is not limited in its application to tax shelter investments. It applies to *any* trade or business activity in which you do not materially participate. To understand just how broad the passive loss rule is, you must understand the term "material participation."

MATERIAL PARTICIPATION

In order to materially participate in an activity, you must be involved in the "operations" of the activity on a "regular, continuous, and substantial" basis. The term "operations" refers to the hands-on conduct of the business. To illustrate the concept of material participation, Congress—no doubt thinking of movie production tax shelters—gives an example of a partnership which produces movies. People who write, read, or select screenplays, Congress says, or who negotiate with agents, or direct, edit, or act in the film, or actively supervise production, are involved in the "operations" of the production company's business. If they are involved on a "regular, continuous and substantial basis," then they materially participate in the activity and are not covered by the passive loss rule. If these people are partners in the partnership, and if the partnership sustains losses, they can use their share of the losses to offset income from any other source. On the other hand, Congress says, people who approve a budget, or accept a recommendation regarding the selection of a screenplay or the choice of an actor, or appoint other people to perform these tasks, are not involved in the "operations" of the business and are covered by the passive loss rules.

In general, Congress says, you are most likely to have material participation in an activity where your involvement in the activity is your principal business or employment. However, Congress does recognize that you might have more than one principal business. Also, according to Congress, you are more likely to have material participation in an activity if you are present at the location where the principal operations of the business are carried on.

Most of us are not involved in movie production companies, so let's consider a more likely scenario. Suppose you are a lawyer or a businessman or a stockbroker who knows a good deal about running a business, but you are principally engaged in your primary occupation. You have a friend or business acquaintance who also is a good businessman but who is not currently employed. You and he decide to open a video store. You will put up the money and he will run the store. You expect the store to lose money at first, so you decide to establish an S corporation, or a general partnership, and go fifty-fifty so that you can each deduct your share of the losses that your store generates in the early years. Your partner goes to the store every day, supervises the employees, deals with the suppliers, keeps the books, promotes the store, and generally manages the business. He reports to you regularly, and you and he discuss strategy, finances, promotion, and pricing, and together you make policy decisions which he then executes. Under these circumstances, according to the tax reform law, your partner is materially participating in the business activity, but you are not. Your partner can deduct his share of the store's losses against any other income, but you are subject to the passive loss rule. That is the impact of the rule.

The same result would probably follow if you owned the store yourself and hired your friend to run it. Without regular, continuous, and substantial participation in the hands-on operation of the business, for you the business is a passive activity covered by the passive loss rule.

RENTAL ACTIVITY

Some businesses run themselves, particularly businesses that consist of renting property, but we are not yet talking about renting real estate property, which is subject to special rules. For example, you may own a sailboat which you rent out under a bareboat charter—that is, you do not provide a crew or any services, just the bare boat. Or you may own some video game machines which you place in pizza parlors or arcades. Or perhaps you own an airplane which you rent under a "dry lease"—no pilots, no fuel, just the plane. These activities do not require a great deal of time on your part, and you might argue that your "participation" in these activities is as "material" as it needs to be and, therefore, you are not subject to the passive loss rules. But Congress thought of that, too; under tax reform a rental activity is generally treated as a passive activity regardless of how relatively material your efforts are.

If you are in the car rental business, or if you own a store which rents video tapes, don't fret.

Congress provided an exception to the passive loss rule for rental businesses which do in fact require a great deal of effort on your part. Where the property you rent is used for a short period of time, with heavy turnover among your customers as in video tape rentals, your business is not a "rental activity" subject to the passive loss rules. However, if someone else runs your store and you do not materially participate in the operation of it, it will be considered a passive activity with respect to you.

Congress also provided that if your business offers substantial services in connection with the rental of property, then it is not a "rental activity." In addition, a rental business is not a passive activity if the cost of the day-to-day operations is not insignificant in comparison to the amount of rental income. Under these rules, a car rental business requiring both substantial services, such as cleaning and maintaining the cars, and high day-to-day costs of operations, such as office rent and mechanics, or a television rental business requiring salesmen and store rent, are not passive activities. A rental activity that is subject to the passive loss rule regardless of your participation in it is one that simply does not require much effort on your part, doesn't cost much to run, and generates a high amount of income in comparison to the cost of running it.

REAL ESTATE RENTAL ACTIVITIES

The passive loss rule applies to real estate rental activities in a special way. Real estate rental activities, like other rental activities, are treated as passive activities subject to the passive loss rule. But even though they are treated as passive, you can still deduct losses from your real estate rental activities, up to a certain amount, against income from any other source. However, you must meet one important condition: you must "actively" participate in your real estate rental activity.

Active participation

"Active participation" in a real estate activity is different from "material participation" in other activities. But then, nobody said that tax reform simplified the tax laws. "Active participation" in real estate rentals does not mean "regular, continuous, and substantial" involvement in operations. It means something less than that. It means that you genuinely participate in the making of "management decisions" or in arranging for other people to provide services. You participate in the making of "management decisions" if you approve new tenants, or decide on the terms of the lease, or approve expenditures for repairs to your property. Arranging for other people to provide services means hiring someone to do the repairs, or to come in and clean the property periodically or tend to the garden.

It appears that you can meet the "active participation" test if *either* you participate in management decisions *or* you arrange for people to provide services. For example, suppose you own an apartment that you rent. You could hire a real estate agent to find tenants and to arrange for whatever repair or other services that the apartment requires. As long as you approve the tenants, set the terms of the lease, and approve the amounts of money that are to be paid for repairs, then you are "actively participating" in your real estate rental activity even if you never show the apartment or call the repairman. Also, it appears that even if the real estate agent decides on his own who is to rent the apartment and under what terms, you are still an "active participant" in your real estate rental activity if you arrange for cleaning and repairs. Exactly how these rules are applied will be worked out in IRS regulations and by court decisions. However, one thing is clear: if you turn the whole affair over to a real estate agent and say, "Just send me the rent after you've paid the bills," then you are not an active participant.

Until clear rules are hammered out, the smart real estate investor will play it safe. He will work with his real estate agent. He will decide what to charge as rent. He will check out the references of his tenant. He will decide whether repairs are necessary and have his real estate agent provide him with bids for the work. He will approve the contractors and other people who will service his rental property. That way, he will be sure to be an active participant.

Two small points before we leave "active participation": You can never be an active participant if you own less than a 10% interest in the real estate. And you can never be an active participant if you invest in real estate as a limited partner in a real estate partnership.

What if you are an active participant?

If you do actively participate in your real estate rental activity, then, even though it is by definition a passive activity, you can still use up to $25,000 of losses from it to offset your salary, dividends, or other income. Your real estate losses must first be used to offset income from other passive activities, such as other real estate rental income or income from your video store (the one that your partner runs). But whatever loss remains may then be used to reduce your salary or dividends or other income, up to $25,000. Suppose your real estate investment generates a loss of $30,000 for the year, and your video store, or a tax shelter that you invested in years ago, throws off $5,000 in income. The $30,000 in real estate losses must first be applied against the $5,000 in video store income, leaving $25,000 in real estate losses. But then that remaining $25,000 real estate loss may be applied against your salary or other income. However, $25,000 is the limit. If the real estate loss was $35,000 instead of $30,000, after applying it against the video store income you would have a remaining real estate loss of $30,000, but only $25,000 of that loss could be used to offset your salary.

There is one more catch to this $25,000 rule. The amount of losses that you can claim under the $25,000 rule declines when your adjusted gross income passes $100,000. For every dollar of adjusted gross income in excess of $100,000, the amount of losses you can claim under the $25,000 rule declines by 50 cents. So if your adjusted gross income is $120,000, the $25,000 rule becomes a $15,000 rule—and $15,000 is the most salary or other income that can be offset with real estate losses. If your adjusted gross income is $150,000 or more, the $25,000 rule doesn't apply to you at all, and all your real estate losses are subject to the passive loss rule.

"PORTFOLIO" INCOME

We have said that losses from a passive activity cannot be used to offset your salary, dividends, or other income, but that they can only be applied against income from other passive activities. You may be wondering why income from your stocks and bonds or saving accounts is not considered income from a passive activity against which losses from a passive activity can be applied. Remember, when we say "passive activity" we mean "passive *trade or business* activity." Dividend income, capital gains from the sale of your stock, and interest income are not "trade or business" income. Such income is called "portfolio income" and, for purposes of the passive loss rule, it is treated just like salary. Losses from a passive trade or business activity cannot be applied against it. By the same token, any losses that you suffer when you sell stocks or bonds are not subject to the passive loss rules and are deductible within the limits of the capital loss rules (see Chapter 9).

Suppose you are a limited partner in a partnership whose only business is to invest in assets that generate dividend and interest income and capital gains. Didn't we say that a limited partnership interest is always a passive activity? Can you now apply tax shelter partnership losses against the income from this investment partnership? Clearly not. The investment partnership income is still "portfolio" income. It has to be this way. Otherwise, everyone would take all of their assets that generate interest, dividends, and capital gains and place them into investment limited partnerships—which the tax shelter promoters would be happy to establish— and then apply their tax shelter or other passive activity losses against the income of those partnerships. Also, if a tax shelter partnership that is engaged in some other businesses happens to generate interest or dividend income as well, that income will be treated as portfolio income unless it is directly related to the business of the partnership, and it cannot be used to absorb partnership expenses. This rule prevents people from putting large amounts of excess cash into a partnership—cash which the partnership does not need to run its business but which is to be used solely to generate income against which partnership expenses can be claimed.

WHAT HAPPENS TO ALL THOSE LOSSES YOU CAN'T USE?

We have seen that losses from a passive activity cannot be used to offset salary or portfolio income, but only income from other passive activities. Real estate losses can be applied against salary or portfolio income within limits—but otherwise only against income from other passive activities. What happens in a year that you don't have any income from other passive activities, or at least not enough income to use up all those passive losses? Are the tax benefits of the losses forfeited forever? Not at all.

Think back to the capital loss carryover rules. After you'd applied your capital losses against your capital gains, and after you'd offset up to $3,000 of your other ordinary income with your excess capital losses, you had capital loss *carryovers*. You stored those losses away and brought them out in the next year, or the year after, to apply them against capital gains in the later year or to offset another $3,000 in ordinary income. You can do the same thing with passive losses.

Passive losses that you can't use in one year are carried over to the next year and the following years until you use them up. These passive losses that are carried forward are called "suspended losses." If your passive activities start to generate income in a later year, you can reduce that income by suspended passive losses from a previous year. Moreover, once you sell your interest in an activity that has generated suspended losses, you can then claim any losses that you haven't been able to use by that time. Once you sell your interest in a passive activity, you are able to determine your overall gain or loss from the activity; and if, overall, you have suffered a loss, you may deduct the overall loss in the year of sale from income from any source. Your suspended losses are used first to offset any income from that passive activity for the year in which you sell it, or to offset any gain that you have on the sale itself.

Next, your suspended losses are applied against any income from other passive activities in the year of the sale, or against any gain on the sale of other passive activities. Finally, if any suspended loss remains, you may offset it against any other income—salary, dividends, interest, or other income. For example, say that you invested $15,000 in a passive activity which generated a loss of $30,000 in one year which you couldn't claim, and in the next year you used $5,000 of that suspended loss to offset income from that activity or from another passive activity, leaving $25,000 of suspended losses. In the following year you sold your interest for $15,000 so that you had no gain or loss from the sale of your investment in the activity. Your remaining suspended losses of $25,000 could be applied first against income or gains from any other passive activities, and then against any other income. If you had sold your interest in the passive activity for $20,000 instead of $15,000, your $25,000 in remaining suspended losses would be used first to offset your $5,000 gain on the sale. This would leave $20,000 in suspended losses to be applied first against income or gain from other passive activities, then against any other income.

Effective date and phase-in rules

As a general rule, the limitations on losses from passive activities apply to losses incurred after December 31, 1986. However, if you purchased or acquired an interest in a passive activity on or prior to October 22, 1986 (the date of enactment of the tax reform act), the passive loss rule is phased in with respect to losses from that activity. We saw this phase-in rule before when we examined the repeal of the deduction for consumer interest (in Chapter 3). As with consumer interest, 65% of the losses from a pre-October 22, 1986, activity that are incurred in 1987 are deductible from salary and portfolio income notwithstanding the passive loss rule—and the other 35% of the losses are subject to the passive loss rule. For losses from a pre-October 22, 1986 activity that are incurred in 1988, 40% are deductible outright and 60% are subject to the passive loss rule; for 1989, 20% are deductible outright and 80% are subject to the passive loss rule; and for 1990, 10% are deductible and 90% are subject to the passive loss rule. All losses incurred in 1991 and later from a passive activity that you invested in prior to October 22, 1986 are subject to the passive loss rule.

Losses from passive activities purchased *after* October 22, 1986 are fully subject to the passive loss rule, starting in 1987. Note that losses incurred during 1986 are not subject to the passive loss rule at all, regardless of when you purchased an interest in the passive activity, because the passive loss rules don't apply until 1987.

It will come as no surprise that these phase-in

rules can get very, very complicated. For example, suppose that, in 1987, you have a $1,000 loss from a pre-October 22, 1986 activity. In 1987, $650 of that loss is deductible from any income, while $350 of it is a passive loss deductible only against income from another passive activity. Now suppose in 1987 you do have income from another passive activity, say $300. Which part of the loss is to be used to offset this $300 in passive activity income? The $650 which is not subject to the passive loss rule? Or the $350 loss that is subject to the passive loss rule? Obviously you would prefer to apply $300 of the $350 portion of the loss, which can be used only to offset passive activity income, against the $300 in passive income and use the $650 portion of the loss to offset your salary. The answer? There is no clear answer. Congress doesn't say what to do. It appears that you could claim the full $650 against your salary and use $300 of the $350 passive loss to offset the $300 in income from the other passive activity, but the IRS may have a different viewpoint. No doubt there are many other unanswerable questions on the application of the passive loss rule.

Earlier we said that special passive loss rules applied to oil and gas investments. The passive loss rules do not apply to "working interests" in oil and gas unless your interest is a limited partnership interest or another type of ownership interest in which your personal liability is limited. A "working interest" in oil and gas is the kind of interest you acquire when you put up money to drill for oil and gas. The tax benefit that you get is the intangible drilling cost deduction. As long as your liability is not limited by your form of ownership, losses that you sustain from a working interest in oil and gas are deductible.

THE ALTERNATIVE MINIMUM TAX

People who invest in tax shelters are often faced with paying tax under the alternative minimum tax. Under the alternative minimum tax, Congress says, in effect, "If we can't tax your income because of all your deductions, we are going to tax your deductions." Under the alternative minimum tax, generally you start with your taxable income and you add back to it many of the deductions that you claimed in figuring out your taxable income, to arrive at your alternative minimum taxable income. After claiming an exemption of $40,000 ($30,000 for single people), the alternative minimum tax rate is applied. If the tax computed in this manner turns out to be more than your regular tax liability, you pay the higher alternative minimum tax. Before tax reform the alternative minimum tax rate was 20%. After tax reform, it is 21%.

Tax reform has also changed the amount of the exemption for some people. The basic exemption amount was $40,000 before tax reform and it still is $40,000 (or $30,000 for single people) as a general rule. However, if your alternative minimum taxable income exceeds $150,000 ($112,500 for single people), the amount of the exemption declines. For each dollar of alternative minimum taxable income above $150,000 (or $112,500), the exemption declines 25 cents. Once alternative minimum taxable income reaches $310,000 ($232,500 for single people), you are entitled to no exemption in calculating your alternative minimum tax.

Tax reform made other changes in the complex minimum tax rules: you will need professional help to deal with them.

CHAPTER FOURTEEN

INVESTMENT INTEREST DEDUCTIONS

Under the tax laws interest that you pay on loans is divided into four categories. One category is home mortgage interest, and in Chapter 3 we saw that home mortgage interest from up to two homes is fully deductible as long as the mortgage on a home isn't greater than what you paid for the property. A second category of interest under the tax laws is consumer interest—interest paid on loans incurred for personal (as opposed to business or investment) purposes. Deductions for consumer interest, under tax reform, are being phased out over the next four years and eventually will not be deductible at all.

A third category of interest is interest paid on loans incurred in your trade or business. Business interest is deductible without limitation. If you borrow money to start a store or a profession, or to expand your business, or simply because your business needs cash, interest that you pay on the borrowings is fully deductible.

And then there is interest paid on money borrowed to make investments—so-called "investment interest". There have always been restrictions on how much investment interest you can deduct. Under tax reform, the restrictions are greater.

What is investment interest?

Investment interest, under the tax code, is interest that you pay on indebtedness which you incur to purchase or carry property which you hold for investment. A clear example is the money you may borrow from a bank to buy a stock; the interest that you pay on that loan is investment interest. Another example is the loan you make to buy art or antiques as an investment; the interest that you pay on the loan is investment interest.

Note that you need not necessarily have borrowed money for an investment in order to have investment interest. Sometimes interest on a loan that is taken out so that you can hold onto an investment is treated as investment interest. For example, if you needed money to pay for a child's vacation abroad and, rather than sell your stock, you borrowed the vacation money, interest paid on that loan might be viewed as investment interest, particularly if you could have sold the stock at a profit. Note also that interest on a debt which is *continued* so that you can make an investment may also be investment interest. For example, if you choose not to repay a business loan so that you can buy some stock with the money that would otherwise have gone to repay the loan, you may have converted business interest into investment interest.

Before tax reform, the amount of investment interest that you could deduct depended only in part on the amount of income that you derived from your investments. The amount of investment interest that you could deduct could go as high as your "net investment income" plus $10,000. You could apply investment interest to reduce your net investment income to zero, and then you could use an additional $10,000 in investment interest to offset income from any other source. Your "net investment income" is the amount of income you earn from your investments less all the expenses—other than interest—incurred in earning it. Therefore, if you bought and sold stock on margin during the year, paid $1,000 for it and sold it for $2,000, paid commissions of $100, and had no other investment expenses, your net investment income would be $900 ($2,000-$1,000-$100). The largest deduction you could claim for investment interest was $10,900—$900 in income plus $10,000.

After tax reform, the additional $10,000 deduction is no longer permitted. Investment interest can be deducted only against net investment income. In the example above, the most investment interest you could deduct for the year would be $900. Investment interest can no longer be used to offset other income.

CHANGES IN TAX DEDUCTIONS FOR INVESTMENT INTEREST

	PRE-1987	AS OF 1987
Income from stock investment:	$ 1,000	$1,000
Paid stock commission:	100	100
Net investment income:	900	900
Maximum claim for investment interest:	10,900	900

While tax reform places greater restrictions on the deductibility of investment interest, it also removes certain kinds of interest from coverage under the investment interest rules and makes them subject to the passive loss rules, instead. For example, before tax reform, if you borrowed money to purchase real estate as an investment, the interest that you paid on those borrowings was investment interest and subject to the investment interest rules. Under tax reform, however, interest which you pay on money which you borrow to use in a passive activity of your own, such as a real estate or other rental activity, is not investment interest but is subject instead to the limitations of the passive loss rule.

Thus, the deductibility of interest paid on a mortgage taken out to buy investment real estate does not depend on whether you have sufficient investment income. It depends on whether losses from the real estate investment, which would include the interest expense, are deductible under the passive loss rule. On the other hand, interest on money borrowed to purchase an interest in a passive activity, such as a limited partnership interest or stock in an S corporation, is apparently still investment interest under tax reform, although the rule is not altogether clear. The interest paid by a partnership in which you are a limited partner, which used to be fully deductible as business interest, will now be subject to the passive loss rule, along with all other partnership deductions.

Effective date and phase-in rules

The new limitation on the deduction of investment interest—the rule that says such interest can only be deducted against investment income—applies to interest paid in 1987 and subsequent years. For 1986, investment interest is allowed against net investment income plus $10,000 of other income. However, like the new consumer interest rules and the passive loss rule, the changes in the investment interest rules are phased in. In 1987, 65% of the interest that you could have claimed if the $10,000 rule had not been repealed is deductible; in 1988, it is 40%; in 1989, 20%; and in 1990, 10%.

Suppose that in 1987 your net investment income is $5,000 and your investment interest expense is $8,000. Before and after tax reform, $5,000 of that interest can be applied against your $5,000 in net investment income. Before tax reform, the remaining $3,000 in investment interest was also deductible, because up to $10,000 in investment interest above net investment income was deductible from other income. Under tax reform, 65% of that $3,000 in excess interest, or $1,950, is deductible in 1987 against other income, but the balance of $1,050 will not be deductible in 1987.

Before tax reform, any investment interest in excess of net investment income plus $10,000 could be carried forward and, subject to the same limitations, claimed in a later year. This carry-forward treatment still applies under tax reform. In our example, therefore, the $1,050 in investment interest not deductible in 1987 can be carried forward to 1988 and applied against net investment income in that year. If it cannot be used in 1988, it can be carried forward to 1989 or later years.

IRA'S AND OTHER PENSION RULES

For several years now, deductions for contributions to individual retirement accounts have been available to practically anyone who was earning a living. The only requirement for claiming an IRA deduction was that your salary or other earned income was at least equal to the amount of the IRA deduction that you claimed.

But it wasn't always so. Prior to 1982, you couldn't claim an IRA deduction if you were covered by a qualified pension plan sponsored by your employer. If you worked for a corporation that had a corporate plan, or if you were self-employed and had a Keogh plan, you were not eligible to make deductible contributions to an IRA. It was only in the Economic Recovery Tax Act of 1981 that Congress first provided that everyone who had earned income could maintain an IRA, regardless of whether they were covered by a corporate plan. With tax reform, we have returned, at least in part, to pre-1982 days.

The tax reform act says that, starting in 1987, you can't make deductible contributions to an IRA if you are an "active participant" in a qualified employer-sponsored plan (corporate or Keogh) unless your income is below a certain level. If your company does not have a qualified plan, or if you do not have a Keogh plan, then obviously you are not an active participant in such a plan and you are free to maintain an IRA, just as you did before tax reform. If your company does have a qualified plan, whether you are an "active participant" in it is not always the easiest thing in the world to determine. We'll come back to that problem later. For now, let's assume that you're an "active participant," and we'll consider the circumstances under which you can make a deductible IRA contribution.

If you are an active participant in an employer's pension plan, then whether you can claim an IRA deduction anyway depends on how much money you earn. If you are married and have an adjusted gross income on your joint return of $40,000 or less, you can claim a full IRA deduction even if you are an active participant. You can put $2,000 into an IRA (or $2,250 if you set up a spousal IRA) and deduct the entire contribution, even if you participate in an employer's plan. However, for each dollar of adjusted gross income above $40,000, your allowable IRA deduction is reduced by 20 cents (for spousal IRA's the allowable deduction is reduced by 22.5 cents). If your adjusted gross income is $45,000, for example, the maximum deductible IRA contribution you can make is $1,000 ($2,000 − .20 × $5,000). Once your joint-return adjusted gross income reaches $50,000, you are permitted no IRA deduction if you are an active participant in an employer-sponsored plan.

For single people and heads of households who are active participants in an employer's plan, this phase-out of the IRA deduction begins at $25,000 and is complete at $35,000.

TAX DEDUCTIBLE IRA CONTRIBUTIONS

	SINGLE PERSON	MARRIED (JOINT RETURN)	HEAD OF HOUSEHOLD
Adjusted gross income not greater than:	$25,000	$40,000	$25,000
Deductible yearly IRA contribution allowed:	2,000	2,000	2,000
Deduction reduced 20¢ for each additional dollar of adjusted gross income up to:	35,000	50,000	35,000

When you are calculating your deductible IRA contribution under this phase-out rule, the allowable IRA deduction can obviously become very small as your adjusted gross income approaches the applicable limits of $50,000 for married people and $35,000 for single people. However, as long as your adjusted gross income is under the applicable limit, you are *always* allowed a deductible IRA contribution of at least $200. If you are single and your adjusted gross income is $34,500, for example, under the phaseout rule your deductible IRA contribution would be $100. Nonetheless, you can still make a $200 deductible contribution to an IRA.

Note that if you are married and file a joint return while *either* you or your spouse is an active participant in a qualified pension plan, then *neither* of you can make deductible IRA contributions unless you are qualified to do so based on your combined adjusted gross income.

When are you an "active participant"?

Whether you are an "active participant" in a qualified plan depends in part on what kind of plan your employer has.

If your employer has a *defined benefit plan*, under which your employer agrees to set aside a sum of money each year which, together with the income earned by that money, will pay you a designated benefit—e.g., $1,000 per month—for as long as you live after retirement, then you are an active participant in that plan as long as you are *eligible* to participate, even if you elect not to. So you can't turn your back on your employer's defined benefit plan in order to set up an IRA.

Suppose your employer has a *defined contribution plan*, under which designated amounts are set aside in an account for you each year and whatever is in that account when you retire is used to fund a retirement benefit. You are an active participant in that plan if any employer contribution to the plan (or forfeitures from other accounts) must be allocated to your account during the plan year that ends with or before your tax year-end (December 31 for most people).

If your employer has a *profit-sharing plan*, under which a portion of any profits for the year are placed into a retirement fund for you and your co-workers to divide up, you are an active participant in any year in which contributions (or forfeitures) are actually allocated to your account.

Once you've become eligible to participate in your employer's defined benefit or defined contribution plan and you work for him throughout the year, you'll be viewed as an active participant. If you leave your employment during the year, you will have to inquire about the terms of the plan to determine whether you were an active participant during the year. For profit sharing plans, "active participant" status will depend on whether your employer had any profits during the year and on whether anyone else forfeited benefits that were allocated to your account—a year-to-year test for profit-sharing plans.

Note that if you are an active participant in a plan under the above rules, the fact that your plan benefits are forfeitable doesn't affect your status as an active participant. In some plans you forfeit benefits that have been set aside for you if you don't work for your employer for a designated period of time. The fact that you risk losing your pension benefits if you change jobs does not make you any less of an active participant as long as you stay on the job.

Nondeductible contributions to IRA's are permitted under tax reform. If you are not permitted to make a deductible contribution to an IRA because you are an active participant in an employer's plan who makes too much money, you can still maintain an IRA and make nondeductible contributions to it. You may contribute up to $2,000 per year as long as you earn that much ($2,250 for spousal IRA's). If, because of the level of your adjusted gross income, you are permitted to make a deductible IRA contribution of something less than $2,000, you can make a nondeductible contribution of the difference between $2,000 and the amount of your deductible contribution. For example, if you were married and filed a joint return and had adjusted gross income of $45,000, you could make a $1,000 *deductible* contribution to an IRA and a $1,000 *nondeductible* contribution. Under tax reform, you can always contribute $2,000 to an IRA—the only question is how much of it is deductible.

Nondeductible contributions to IRA's do not save you taxes when you make them. However, the income that those nondeductible contributions earn is tax-free until you start to draw it down after retirement. If you make a nondeductible IRA contribution, the amount of the contribution itself is not taxable when you draw it down at retirement because you already paid taxes on that contribution—only the income it earns is taxed at that time.

Spousal IRA's

Before tax reform, if you made an IRA contribution for yourself you could also make an additional $250 contribution for your spouse. These IRA's are called "spousal IRA's." However, you could make this additional contribution only if your spouse earned no income. If she (or he) earned income of her (or his) own, she (he) had to start an IRA. Congress decided it didn't make much sense to force spouses who earned less than $250 to set up their own IRA's. Therefore, under tax reform, you can have a spousal IRA even if your spouse does have income. If your spouse joins you in a spousal IRA, however, she cannot have an IRA of her own.

As a practical matter, you will use a spousal IRA only if your spouse earns $250 or less during the year—or if your spouse doesn't want to contribute more than $250 to an IRA even if she earns more than that. If larger contributions are permitted and desired, each spouse will want his or her own IRA. This change in the spousal IRA rules—permitting you to have a spousal IRA even if your spouse has earnings—applies to your 1986 tax return.

Remember, though, that if *either* spouse is covered by an employer plan, *neither* spouse can have a deductible spousal IRA, a deductible regular IRA, or any deductible IRA, unless their combined adjusted gross income is below $50,000. However, you can have a *nondeductible* spousal IRA up to $2,250, less the amount of any deductible IRA contribution you were permitted to make because your adjusted gross income was below $50,000.

If you are wondering why Congress made all these complicated changes in the IRA rules, a little history will help you to understand. Back in 1981, Congress decided to let everybody have an IRA because at the time it was afraid that the Social Security system would collapse before the end of the decade, and it figured that retired people would have to fend for themselves. Then, Congress dramatically increased Social Security taxes, and today the Social Security system is solvent again. So, having increased the Social Security taxes that you pay, Congress can now take away IRA deductions for everybody covered by an employer's pension plan. However, the fact that Congress still permits you to make nondeductible IRA contributions suggests that it is still not altogether confident about the stability of the Social Security system.

Borrowing money for IRA contributions

Many people borrow money to make IRA contributions. They get a deduction for the IRA contribution and then they deduct the interest that they pay on the borrowed funds. Note that interest on such borrowings is *consumer interest* and, after tax reform, the deduction for it is being phased out.

IRA investments in coins

Since 1982, IRA's have been prohibited from investing in collectibles. For some reason, perhaps the art of lobbying in its highest form, the tax reform act says that after 1986, IRA's can invest in gold or silver coins issued by the United States. Investments in stamps, art, antiques, and other collectibles, or in gold or silver bullion, are still prohibited. It appears that stamp merchants and purveyors of gold and silver bullion need to organize!

Early withdrawals from IRA accounts

Tax reform has made it somewhat easier to withdraw money from an IRA, but the changes are nothing to get excited about. Prior to tax reform, you were supposed to take money out of your IRA only when you reached age 59½ or became disabled. Or if you died, your heirs could withdraw the money. Any withdrawals other than these permitted withdrawals were subject to a penalty equal to 10% of the amount of the unauthorized withdrawal.

Under tax reform, there are two additional
circumstances under which you can make an

early withdrawal from an IRA without penalty. One does you no good whatsoever: you can withdraw money from an IRA before attaining age 59½ if a divorce court orders you to give the money to your ex-spouse. The other exception permits you to withdraw money from an IRA if you arrange for a scheduled series of substantially equal periodic payments to be paid throughout your lifetime—in other words, if you convert your IRA account into an annuity.

OTHER PENSION RULES

The tax reform act makes changes not only in the IRA provisions, but also in many other pension-related rules. Here are three changes with broad applicability.

Reduction in allowable contributions to "cash-or-deferred" plans

Under some profit-sharing plans and certain older defined contribution plans, corporate employees can choose between having money put aside on a tax-deferred basis for their retirement or taking the funds currently as taxable compensation. These plans are called "cash-or-deferred" arrangements. Prior to tax reform, an employee could direct that as much as $30,000 per year—but never more than 25% of his compensation—be put aside for his retirement. Under tax reform, the $30,000 limit is reduced to $7,000. This change in the cash-or-deferred rules applies only to plans that permit you to choose between current or deferred compensation, and should not be confused with the allowable contributions to a regular defined contribution plan in which money is only set aside for retirement. Contributions to regular plans can still go as

high as $30,000, or 25% of compensation, which-
ever is less.

Curtailment of loans from qualified corporate plans

Under the pension law, if you borrow money
from a qualified employer's plan in which you
participate, the proceeds of the loan are normally treated as a distribution from the plan
which is taxable to you. However, a taxable
distribution can be avoided if the loan meets
certain requirements.

Prior to tax reform, a loan from a plan was not
a taxable distribution if the amount of the loan
did not exceed 50% of your accrued benefit
under the plan—but you could always borrow at
least $10,000. However, under no circumstances
could the total of your plan loans (including any
previous loans) exceed $50,000, even if 50% of
your accrued benefit was more than $50,000. In
addition, loans had to be repaid within 5 years.
However, if the loan proceeds were used to buy
or improve your principal residence or the residence of a family member, repayment merely
had to occur over a reasonable period of time.

The tax reform act changes these plan rules
with respect to that $50,000 limitation. The
$50,000 limit may be reduced if you have bor-
rowed from the plan during the previous 12
months. The amount of the reduction is determined as follows: you take the highest outstanding balance of plan loans during the previous 12-
month period and reduce it by the outstanding
balance of plan loans on the day that you take
out a new loan from the plan. This difference is
applied to reduce the overall $50,000 limit. Sup-
pose you want to borrow money from your
plan on November 1, 1987. Suppose further
that on February 1, 1987 you borrow $30,000

from the plan and repay it on March 1, 1987. Suppose you then borrow another $10,000 from the plan on May 1, 1987. Before tax reform, you could borrow as much as $40,000 (assuming that 50% of your accured benefit amounted to at least that amount)—the $50,000 limit less the $10,000 loan outstanding.

Under tax reform, however, the most money you can borrow from the plan on November 1, 1987 is $30,000—the $50,000 limit reduced by the difference between your highest outstanding balance during the previous 12-month period ($30,000) and the outstanding balance on the date that you borrow ($10,000), or $50,000 less $20,000. If you want to borrow $40,000 from the plan, you must wait until the following February 1, at which point that highest outstanding balance of $30,000 is more than 12 months old and is no longer taken into account.

Tax reform also changes the rules with respect to repaying plan loans. Loans to purchase your own principal residence can still be repaid over a reasonable period which exceeds five years. All other loans, including loans to improve your residence or to purchase a home for a family member, must now be repaid within 5 years. And under tax reform *all* plan loans must be amortized with level payments which are due at least quarterly. Balloon loans for residences are prohibited.

These plan loan rules apply to loans made after December 31, 1986.

Ten-year averaging is repealed

Prior to tax reform, if you received a lump sum distribution from a pension plan, you could elect to be taxed on this distribution under the "ten-year forward averaging" rule. Under ten-year averaging, the tax paid in the year of distribution was ten times the tax that was due on one-tenth of the distribution. This technique saved you taxes, particularly before most of the tax brackets were repealed, because it kept that lump sum distribution from being taxed at progressively higher tax rates. You obviously preferred to have one-tenth of the distribution taxed ten times at, say, the 25% bracket than to have a portion of it taxed at 28%, another portion at 33%, still another portion at 38%, and so on.

Under tax reform, the ten-year forward averaging rule is replaced by a five-year forward averaging rule—one-fifth of the distribution will now be taxed five times. The five-year rule is less favorable to you, since one-fifth of a distribution is more likely to fall into a higher bracket than one-tenth of a distribution. There is some relief from this change for people nearing retirement. If you had turned 50 years old by January 1, 1986, you can elect to use the old ten-year rule. People who were over 50 on January 1, 1986 should see their tax advisors about this and other changes in the pension law.

CHAPTER SIXTEEN

CHILDREN'S UNEARNED INCOME & FAMILY TRUSTS

Before tax reform, family income splitting had become a popular tax-savings strategy. Those progressive tax brackets were once again responsible. If you earned a large salary and were in the 50% bracket, your interest income and dividends were also subject to a 50% tax. One solution was to give income-producing property to a child who had no substantial amounts of income of his own. Then the income from that property was taxed at 14% or 16% instead of at 50%. If you had more than one child, so much the better. You could spread your income-producing property among several people with low tax brackets.

Even with the elimination of most of the tax brackets under tax reform, family income splitting could have still been used because children would have most of their income taxed at the 15% rate rather than at the 28% or 33% rate. However, the tax reform act of 1986 has put a stop to most family income-splitting strategies.

YOUR CHILD'S INCOME TAX RATES

Under tax reform, most of the unearned income of a child under 14 years of age is taxed as though it was his parents' income—and at his parents' marginal rates. If you give your child income-producing property, and if your income is taxed at the 33% rate, most of the income that your child makes from the property will also be taxed at the 33% rate. Note that this rule applies to *all* of your child's unearned income. If his grandparents give him property which generates income, that income is taxed as though it were yours. If your child wins the lottery, that income is also taxed at the same rate as your own. All of the income which your child makes other than by working is taxed at your highest marginal rate. Your child still files a tax return and reports the income that he makes, but the rates that apply are your highest marginal rates, not the rates that would normally apply. If a child's parents are divorced, his unearned income is taxed at the marginal rates of the parent who has custody.

CAN THE IRS BE ACCUSED OF CHILD ABUSE?

The IRS deals roughly with a child under 14 years of age who has only unearned income. This child gets only $500 as a standard deduction and only another $500 of his unearned income is taxed at his own rates. The remainder of your child's unearned income is taxed at your higher income tax rates. But then, children under 14 can't vote.

Young children are not taxed at your rates on all of their unearned income but only on that portion of it which exceeds a designated amount. We'll return to that shortly. Also, children, like all taxpayers, are not taxed on their *gross* unearned income but on their "taxable" unearned income. Taxable unearned income—like everybody's taxable income—is the total unearned income reduced by allowable deductions. A child's taxable unearned income is determined by reducing his unearned income by one of two amounts. In Chapter 7, we saw that a child could apply $500 of his standard deduction to offset unearned income. That's one amount: a child gets a $500 standard deduction against his unearned income, just as we all get a standard deduction. A child may also have itemized deductions which are directly attributable to the production of unearned income (these would be miscellaneous itemized deductions in the 2% pot)—such as bank fees or portfolio management fees or brokerage fees. That's the second amount. If it is to a child's advantage to claim itemized deductions, this second amount, you will see, is always at least $500. A child's "taxable unearned income" is his unearned income reduced by the larger of these two amounts.

Now, we said that young children are not taxed at your rates on all of their unearned income. To be more precise, young children are not taxed at your rates on all of their *taxable* unearned income. The first $500 of a child's taxable unearned income is taxed at the child's rates, but all taxable unearned income above $500 is taxed at your rates. Therefore, if a child's taxable unearned income is $1,000, $500 is taxed at his rates and $500 is taxed at your rates.

Some examples: Suppose your child has $500 of unearned income and no earned income. Since he can apply $500 of his standard deduction to offset this income, his "taxable unearned income" is zero and it's not taxed at all. Or suppose your child has $1,000 of unearned income and no earned income. He (or she) uses $500 of his standard deduction to arrive at $500 of "taxable unearned income." Since taxable unearned income does not exceed $500, it is all taxed at your child's rates. If he had $1,200 in unearned income and used $500 of his standard deduction, his taxable unearned income would be $700. Of that, $500 would be taxed at his rates and $200 would be taxed at your rates. And if your child had $1,200 in unearned income and $600 in itemized deductions attributable to that income, his taxable unearned income would be $600, of which $500 would be taxed at his rates and $100 at your rates.

Dealing with earned income

The problems start when your child also has

earned income such as that from a paper-route, particularly when it is combined with itemized deductions. Let's start with the presence of paper-route income and no itemized deductions. The question is: do you use the standard deduction to reduce the *earned* income taxable at his rates or to reduce the *unearned* income taxable at your rates? The answer: you use the standard deduction first to reduce up to $500 of unearned income so that as little income as possible will be taxed at your rates. For example, if a child has $700 of earned income and $300 of unearned income, he can claim a standard deduction of $700—the allowable standard deduction is always as much as your child's earned income, up to the limit of the standard deduction, or $2,540 for 1987. This $700 standard deduction is first applied against the $300 of unearned income, eliminating that income entirely. The balance of the standard deduction, or $400, is applied against the $700 of earned income. The child therefore has taxable income of $300, but it is taxable *earned* income that is taxed at the child's rates.

Remember, however, that only $500 of the standard deduction can be used to offset unearned income. Therefore, if your child had $800 of earned income and $800 of unearned income, he would use $500 of his $800 standard deduction to offset unearned income, leaving $300 of taxable unearned income. All of this taxable unearned income would be taxed at your child's rates because the first $500 of taxable unearned income is always taxed at his rates. The remaining standard deduction of $300 would reduce earned income to $500 of taxable earned income. Taxable *earned* income is always taxed at the child's rates.

If your child had $2,000 of unearned income

and $800 of earned income, $500 of the $800 standard deduction would be applied against the unearned income, resulting in $1,500 of taxable unearned income. Of that, $500 would be taxed at his rates and $1,000 would be taxed at your rates. The remaining $300 of standard deduction would be applied against earned income, resulting in $500 of taxable earned income which is always taxed at the child's rates.

Let's turn to itemized deductions

Itemized deductions that are directly allocable to the production of a child's unearned income are applied against unearned income. Itemized deductions not related to unearned income are not applied against unearned income, but against earned income. However, if you don't have at least $500 in itemized deductions that are related to unearned income, you can draw from other itemized deductions to reach the $500 figure. If your child is itemizing deductions, he can always use at least $500 of his itemized deductions to reduce the amount of taxable unearned income that is taxed at your rates.

More examples: Suppose your child has $1,200 of unearned income and $400 of earned income. Suppose, in addition, that he has $800 of itemized deductions, of which $400 are related to unearned income. Since he can always offset unearned income with at least $500 of itemized deductions, whether or not they relate to unearned income, he applies $500 of his itemized deductions against $1,200 of unearned income to arrive at $700 of taxable unearned income. Of that, $500 is taxed at his rates, and $200 is taxed at your rates. The remaining $300 of itemized deductions reduces his $400 of earned income to $100 of taxable earned income—always taxable at your child's rates. Remember that our objective is to subject income to taxation at the child's rate to the extent that the law permits.

Finally, suppose that your child has $2,000 of unearned income, $700 of earned income, and $1,000 of itemized deductions, of which $800 are related to unearned income. Since the itemized deductions related only to unearned income are more than $500, those deductions are applied against unearned income to arrive at $1,200 of taxable unearned income. Of that, $500 is taxed at your child's rates and $700 at your rates. The $200 in itemized deductions not related to unearned income are applied against earned income, resulting in $500 of taxable earned income, which is always taxed at your child's rates. Naturally, you would prefer to apply all the itemized deductions against unearned income to further reduce the amount of that income which is taxed at your rates. But you can't do that. You can only offset unearned income with *related* itemized deductions unless those related itemized deductions are less than $500, in which case you can draw from other itemized deductions to get up to $500.

These unearned income rules for your child are by no means simple. But don't get confused about whether your child should claim the standard deduction or itemized deductions. The rules are designed so that, like all taxpayers, your child *always* claims itemized deductions if the amount of the itemized deductions exceeds the allowable standard deduction, regardless of whether those itemized deductions are related to unearned income. It works out that way because your child offsets unearned income *either* by $500 of the standard deduction *or* by $500 of itemized deductions whether or not they relate to unearned income. Therefore, if itemized deductions exceed the allowable standard deduction, it is always to your child's advantage to claim them. Either way, his unearned income—the income subject to tax at your rates—is always reduced by at least $500, and the remaining itemized deductions can be applied against earned income.

If you feel that these rules are unnecessarily complex just to squeeze a few more dollars in taxes out of your child, write your congressman.

TRUSTS

For tax purposes, most trusts are separate "people." They calculate their own taxable income and pay tax on that income at their own rates. Like regular people, before tax reform the trusts had 14 tax brackets to deal with in figuring out their tax. Tax reform has simplified life for trusts, too. Under tax reform, a trust's income is taxed at two brackets—the 15% and the 28% bracket—and at the secret 33% bracket. Beginning in 1988, the first $5,000 of a trust's income is taxed at the 15% rate. Everything above that is taxed at the 28% rate, except that at $13,000 of taxable income the 33% rate comes into effect and continues to apply until taxable income reaches $26,000, at which point the benefit of the 15% rate has been eliminated.

Trusts claim a standard deduction of $100—or $300 if the trust is required to distribute all of its income. They don't get a personal exemption. These rules don't change under tax reform.

Prior to tax reform, trusts were permitted to use a taxable year-end of their choice—March 31, July 31, December 31, as they elected. Under the tax reform act, trusts must use a taxable year which ends on October 31, November 30, or December 31. Existing trusts which use a different year-end will have to change to a permissible year-end in 1987.

GRANTOR TRUSTS

The tax law has always made it difficult for you to divert income to a trust, so that the income could be taxed at a lower rate, while at the same time reserving for yourself the right to enjoy that income. Under the tax law, the general rule is that if you transfer property to a trust and retain designated rights in that property, then the trust is disregarded for tax purposes and its income is taxed on your return as though you earned it yourself.

One of those designated rights which has always resulted in the trust being disregarded is the right to get the property back. If you set up a revocable trust that you can later dismantle in order to retrieve the property you put into it, the trust is disregarded for tax purposes. Also, if you have the right under the trust document to have the income of the trust paid to you, the trust is disregarded. These trusts from which either corpus or income can be retrieved are called "grantor trusts," and all of their income is taxed to the person who established them.

Prior to tax reform, there was an exception to "grantor trust" treatment if the trust was irrevocable for more than 10 years. If you couldn't retrieve the property or claim the income it generated for more than 10 years, the trust was recognized for tax purposes during that period when you couldn't touch principal or income— and the trust filed its own tax return and reported its income. Under tax reform, this "more than 10 years" exception is repealed. If you set up a trust and you can *ever* reclaim the principal or the income, the trust will be disregarded for tax purposes. There is one exception to the tax reform change. If the beneficiary of the trust is a child or other lineal descendant, and if you may reclaim corpus or income only if he dies before reaching age 21, then the trust will be recognized for tax purposes. Otherwise, for the trust to be recognized as a separate person, you must part with the property that you put into it, and the income that it generates, forever.

Even if you set up a totally irrevocable trust, you will still be taxed on its income if you retain certain other rights or powers with respect to the trust. If you retain the power to decide who enjoys the income of the trust, the trust will be disregarded for tax purposes. If you have the sole power to deal with the trust's assets on a less than arm's-length basis, the trust will be disregarded for tax purposes. Or if you borrow money from the trust at a favorable interest rate and don't provide security for the loan, the trust will be disregarded for tax purposes. These rules have always applied to trusts, but before tax reform you could give to your spouse many of the rights or powers that you were prohibited from holding yourself. The new tax law has changed that. Under tax reform, if your spouse holds any of the rights or powers that you cannot hold yourself, the trust will be disregarded for tax purposes.

In summary, if you want to set up a trust as a separate person for tax purposes, it must be totally irrevocable, and you and your spouse must not retain any significant powers or rights with respect to the administration of the trust or the enjoyment of its income. The changes in the grantor trust rules apply to transfers in trust made after March 1, 1986.

AFTERWORD

In Chapter 1 we stated that, in the interest of simplification, Congress repealed many of the tax brackets, set lower tax rates, and limited the use of, or repealed, many deductions. Now we see that we still have a very complex tax system. After tax reform the tax laws may or may not be fairer, but they certainly aren't noticeably simpler and, for many people, they are far more complex.

"Fairness" in the tax law comes in more than one color. Everyone paying his fair share of tax is one kind of fairness. Whether tax reform achieves that goal remains to be seen. Another kind of fairness is an understandable tax system. Surely it is unfair that the law is so complex that you must pay someone to help you complete a tax return which you are required to file, or that you are penalized by the IRS for making mistakes on a tax return which, according to surveys, most IRS agents would also make. Tax reform does very little, perhaps nothing, to remove this kind of unfairness.

Cutting 14 brackets to 2 brackets, while making it somewhat easier to do a quick approximation of what your tax will be, does not simplify the tax laws at all. True simplification comes when it is easier to determine your taxable income. Tax reform, if anything, makes it harder to do that.

The 1986 Tax Reform Act is the sixth major tax revision in ten years (major tax bills were enacted in 1976, 1978, 1981, 1982 and 1984). Recurring changes in the tax laws do not contribute to simplification, either. They make it more difficult for the IRS to write regulations which interpret the law, which in turn makes it more difficult for tax advisors to tell their clients what the law means, which in turn makes it more difficult for the clients—that is, taxpayers—to understand what the tax consequences of their actions are. Tax reform, with its lower rates, was supposed to make the tax consequences of your actions less important, but we have seen that a 33% rate still applies to a large portion of many people's incomes—and that is enough tax to make tax consequences matter. Tax reform, by making complicated changes in the tax law for the sixth time in ten years, may have simply made a flawed system worse.

The solution? At one point in its deliberations on tax reform, Congress may have lit upon the solution. The Senate bill called for an informal understanding by the Congress that, after the 1986 legislation was enacted, there would be no more major tax legislation for at least five years. This measure was deleted from the bill before final passage. Its deletion tells us that many congressmen feared that major portions of the bill were bad law and wanted the leeway to be able to make still more changes or even repeal what they had done. But at some point this process has to stop.

Americans have proven skillful at adapting to any law, if only given enough time. Perhaps it is time to give us time—to take tax reform, the good and the bad, and live with it for a while. The tax law has become like the weather in New England—unpredictable. An unpredictable tax system, molded by the whims of congressmen and by changing notions of what is fair, is perhaps the least fair system of all.

TAX REFORM AND YOUR TAX RETURN

Form **1040** Department of the Treasury—Internal Revenue Service
U.S. Individual Income Tax Return 1986 (2)

For the year January 1–December 31, 1986, or other tax year beginning _____ , 1986, ending _____ , 19 ____ | OMB No. 1545-0074

Use IRS label. Other-wise, please print or type.	Your first name and initial (if joint return, also give spouse's name and initial) · Last name · **Your social security number**
	Present home address (number and street or rural route) (If you have a P.O. Box, see page 4 of Instructions.) · **Spouse's social security number**
	City, town or post office, state, and ZIP code · If this address is different from the one shown on your 1985 return, check here ▶ ☐

Presidential Election Campaign ▶ Do you want $1 to go to this fund? · Yes ☐ No ☐ | **Note:** Checking "Yes" will not change your tax or reduce your refund
If joint return, does your spouse want $1 to go to this fund? · Yes ☐ No ☐

For Privacy Act and Paperwork Reduction Act Notice, see Instructions

Filing Status

Check only one box.

1 ☐ Single
2 ☐ Married filing joint return (even if only one had income)
3 ☐ Married filing separate return. Enter spouse's social security no. above and full name here. ____
4 ☐ Head of household (with qualifying person). (See page 5 of Instructions.) If the qualifying person is your unmarried child but not your dependent, enter child's name here. ____
5 ☐ Qualifying widow(er) with dependent child (year spouse died ▶ 19 ____). (See page 6 of Instructions.)

Exemptions

Always check the box labeled Yourself.
Check other boxes if they apply

6a ☐ Yourself   ☐ 65 or over   ☐ Blind } Enter number of boxes checked on 6a and b ▶
 b ☐ Spouse   ☐ 65 or over   ☐ Blind

c First names of your dependent children who lived with you ____   Enter number of children listed on 6c ▶

d First names of your dependent children who did not live with you (see page 6) ____
(If pre-1985 agreement, check here ▶ ☐.)   Enter number of children listed on 6d ▶

e Other dependents:

(1) Name	(2) Relationship	(3) Number of months lived in your home	(4) Did dependent have income of $1,080 or more?	(5) Did you provide more than one-half of dependent's support?

Enter number of other dependents ▶

f Total number of exemptions claimed (also complete line 36) · Add numbers entered in boxes above ▶

7 Wages, salaries, tips, etc. (attach Form(s) W-2)

THESE ARE WORTH MORE, IF YOU DON'T MAKE TOO MUCH MONEY. (CHAPTER SEVEN)

SOCIAL SECURITY NUMBERS WILL BE REQUIRED, TOO. (CHAPTER SEVEN)

REPEALED! (CHAPTER TWO)

ALL OF YOUR LONG-TERM CAPITAL GAINS WILL NOW BE INCLUDED HERE. (CHAPTER NINE)

LOSSES ARE SUBJECT TO THE PASSIVE LOSS RULE. (CHAPTER THIRTEEN)

IT'S ALL TAXED NOW. (CHAPTER TWO)

YOU MUST INCLUDE SCHOLARSHIP MONEY FOR ROOM AND BOARD, AND PRIZES AND AWARDS. (CHAPTER TWO)

AN ITEMIZED DEDUCTION. (CHAPTER THREE)

AN ITEMIZED DEDUCTION THAT GOES INTO THE 2% POT. (CHAPTER FIVE)

NOT ALLOWED IF YOU ARE COVERED BY YOUR EMPLOYER'S PLAN, UNLESS YOUR INCOME IS BELOW A CERTAIN LEVEL. (CHAPTER FIFTEEN)

REPEALED! (CHAPTER ONE)

Please attach Copy B of your Forms W-2, W-2G, and W-2P here.

If you do not have a W-2, see page 4 of Instructions.

Please attach check or money order here.

Adjustments to Income (See Instructions on page 11.)

Adjusted Gross Income

9a Dividends *(also attach Schedule B if over $400)*	,	9b Exclusion
c Subtract line 9b from line 9a and enter the result		9c
10 Taxable refunds of state and local income taxes, if any, from the worksheet on page 9 of Instructions.		10
11 Alimony received		11
12 Business income or (loss) *(attach Schedule C)*		12
13 Capital gain or (loss) *(attach Schedule D)*		13
14 40% of capital gain distributions not reported on line 13 *(see page 9 of Instructions)*		14
15 Other gains or (losses) *(attach Form 4797)*		15
16 Fully taxable pensions, IRA distributions, and annuities not reported on line 17 (see page 9).		16
17a Other pensions and annuities, including rollovers. Total received 17a		17b
b Taxable amount, if any, from the worksheet on page 10 of Instructions		18
18 Rents, royalties, partnerships, estates, trusts, etc. *(attach Schedule E)*		
19 Farm income or (loss) *(attach Schedule F)*		19
20a Unemployment compensation (insurance). Total received 20a		20b
b Taxable amount, if any, from the worksheet on page 10 of Instructions		
21a Social security benefits (see page 10). 21a	Tax exempt interest	21b
b Taxable amount, if any, from worksheet on page 11 of Instructions		
22 Other income (list type and amount—see page 11 of Instructions)		22
23 Add the amounts shown in the far right column for lines 7 through 22. This is your **total income** ▶		23
24 Moving expenses *(attach Form 3903 or 3903F)*	24	
25 Employee business expenses *(attach Form 2106)*	25	
26 IRA deduction, from the worksheet on page 12	26	
27 Keogh retirement plan and self-employed SEP deduction	27	
28 Penalty on early withdrawal of savings	28	
29 Alimony paid (recipient's last name _____ and social security no. _____)	29	
30 Deduction for a married couple when both work *(attach Schedule W)*	30	
31 Add lines 24 through 30. These are your **total adjustments** ▶		31
32 Subtract line 31 from line 23. This is your **adjusted gross income**. If this line is less than $11,000 and a child lived with you, see "Earned Income Credit" (line 58) on page 16 of Instructions. If you want IRS to figure your tax, see page 13 of Instructions ▶		32

Tax Computation

(See Instructions on page 13.)

33	Amount from line 32 (adjusted gross income)	33
34a	If you itemize, attach Schedule A (Form 1040) and enter the amount from Schedule A, line 26	34a
	Caution: If you have unearned income and can be claimed as a dependent on your parents' return, see page 13 of Instructions and check here ▶ ☐ . Also see page 13 if you are married filing a separate return and your spouse itemizes deductions, or you are a dual-status alien.	
b	If you do not itemize but you made charitable contributions, enter your cash contributions here. (If you gave $3,000 or more to any one organization, see page 14.)	34b
c	Enter your noncash contributions (you must attach Form 8283 if over $500)	34c
d	Add lines 34b and 34c. Enter the total	34d
35	Subtract line 34a or line 34d, whichever applies, from line 33	35
36	Multiply $1,080 by the total number of exemptions claimed on line 6f (see page 14)	36
37	**Taxable income.** Subtract line 36 from line 35. Enter the result (but not less than zero)	37
38	Enter tax here. Check if from ☐ Tax Table, ☐ Tax Rate Schedule X, Y, or Z, or ☐ Schedule G	38
39	Additional taxes (see page 14 of Instructions). Enter here and check if from ☐ Form 4970, ☐ Form 4972, or ☐ Form 5544	39
40	Add lines 38 and 39. Enter the total	40

Credits

(See Instructions on page 14.)

41	Credit for child and dependent care expenses (attach Form 2441)	41
42	Credit for the elderly or for the permanently and totally disabled (attach Schedule R)	42
43	Partial credit for political contributions for which you have receipts	43
44	Add lines 41 through 43. Enter the total	44
45	Subtract line 44 from line 40. Enter the result (but not less than zero)	45
46	Foreign tax credit (attach Form 1116)	46
47	General business credit. Check if from ☐ Form 3800, ☐ Form 3468, ☐ Form 5884, ☐ Form 6478, or ☐ Form 6765	47
48	Add lines 46 and 47. Enter the total	48
49	Subtract line 48 from line 45. Enter the result (but not less than zero)	49

Other

50	Self-employment tax (attach Schedule SE)	50

EXPIRED. (CHAPTER THREE)

A LINE FOR THE STANDARD DEDUCTION WILL BE BACK. (CHAPTER FOUR)

$1,900 FOR 1987, $1,950 FOR 1988, $2,000 FOR 1989, THEN ADJUSTED FOR INFLATION. (CHAPTER SEVEN)

ONLY TWO BRACKETS PER SCHEDULE, PLUS THE SECRET 33% BRACKET. (CHAPTER ONE)

INCOME AVERAGING IS REPEALED. (CHAPTER ONE)

Social security tax on tip income not reported to employer (attach Form 4137)

(CHAPTER EIGHT)

53

54 Tax on an IRA (attach Form 5329) · · · · · · · · · · · 54

55 Add lines 49 through 54. This is your **total tax** · · · · · ▶ 55

(Including Advance EIC Payments)

Payments

Attach Forms W-2, W-2G, and W-2P to front.

56 Federal income tax withheld · · · · · · · 56

57 1986 estimated tax payments and amount applied from 1985 return 57

INVESTMENT TAX CREDIT IS REPEALED. (CHAPTER EIGHT)

58 Earned income credit (see page 16) · · · · 58

59 Amount paid with Form 4868 · · · · · · · 59

60 Excess social security tax and RRTA tax withheld (two or more employers) 60

NOW 21% (CHAPTER THIRTEEN)

61 Credit for Federal tax on gasoline and special fuels (attach Form 4136) 61

62 Regulated investment company credit (attach Form 2439) 62

63 Add lines 56 through 62. These are your **total payments** · · · ▶ 63

Refund or Amount You Owe

64 If line 63 is larger than line 55, enter amount **OVERPAID** · · · ▶ 64

65 Amount of line 64 to be **REFUNDED TO YOU** · · · · · · · ▶ 65

66 Amount of line 64 to be applied to your 1987 estimated tax ▶ 66

67 If line 55 is larger than line 63, enter **AMOUNT YOU OWE.** Attach check or money order for full amount payable to "Internal Revenue Service." Write your social security number, daytime phone number, and "1986 Form 1040" on it · · · · · **Penalty:** $ ▶ 67

Check ▶ ☐ if Form 2210 (2210F) is attached See page 17

Please Sign Here

Under penalties of perjury, I declare that I have examined this return and accompanying schedules and statements, and to the best of my knowledge and belief, they are true, correct, and complete. Declaration of preparer (other than taxpayer) is based on all information of which preparer has any knowledge.

▶ Your signature | Date | Your occupation

▶ Spouse's signature (if joint return, BOTH must sign) | Date | Spouse's occupation

Paid Preparer's Use Only

Preparer's signature | Date | Check if self-employed ☐ | Preparer's social security no.

Firm's name (or yours, if self-employed) and address ▶ | E.I. No. | ZIP code

SCHEDULES A&B (Form 1040)

Schedule A—Itemized Deductions
(Schedule B is on back)

▶ Attach to Form 1040. ▶ See Instructions for Schedules A and B (Form 1040).

Department of the Treasury
Internal Revenue Service (2)

Name(s) as shown on Form 1040

Your social security number

Medical and Dental Expenses (Do not include expenses reimbursed or paid by others.) (See Instructions on page 19.)	**1** Prescription medicines and drugs; and insulin	1
	2 a Doctors, dentists, nurses, hospitals, insurance premiums you paid for medical and dental care, etc.	2a
	b Transportation and lodging	2b
	c Other (list—include hearing aids, dentures, eyeglasses, etc.) ▶	2c
	3 Add lines 1 through 2c, and enter the total here	3
	4 Multiply the amount on Form 1040, line 33, by 5% (.05)	4
	5 Subtract line 4 from line 3. If zero or less, enter -0-. **Total** medical and dental ▶	5
Taxes You Paid (See Instructions on page 20.)	**6** State and local income taxes	6
	7 Real estate taxes	7
	8 a General sales tax (see sales tax tables in instruction booklet)	8a
	b General sales tax on motor vehicles	8b
	9 Other taxes (list—include personal property taxes) ▶	9
	10 Add the amounts on lines 6 through 9. Enter the total here. **Total taxes** ▶	10
Interest You Paid (See Instructions on	**11 a** Home mortgage interest paid to financial institutions (report deductible points on line 13)	11a
	b Home mortgage interest you paid to individuals (show that person's name and address) ▶	11b
	12	12

NOW 7½%.
(CHAPTER THREE)

REPEALED.
(CHAPTER THREE)

SUBJECT TO THE PURCHASE PRICE RULE. (CHAPTER THREE)

REPEALED.

	13		

14 Add the amounts on lines 11a through 13. Enter the total here. **Total interest** ▶ | **14** |

Contributions You Made

(See Instructions on page 21.)

15 a Cash contributions. (If you gave $3,000 or more to any one organization, report those contributions on line 15b.) | **15a** |

b Cash contributions totaling $3,000 or more to any one organization. (Show to whom you gave and how much you gave.) ▶ .... | **15b** |

16 Other than cash. (You must attach Form 8283 if over $500.) . | **16** |

17 Carryover from prior year . . . . | **17** |

18 Add the amounts on lines 15a through 17. Enter the total here. **Total contributions** ▶ | **18** |

Casualty and Theft Losses

19 Total casualty or theft loss(es). (You must attach Form 4684 or similar statement.) (See page 21 of Instructions.) . . . . ▶ | **19** |

Miscellaneous Deductions

(See Instructions on page 22.)

20 Union and professional dues . . . . | **20** |

21 Tax return preparation fee . . . . | **21** |

22 Other (list type and amount) ▶ ....
....
.... | **22** |

23 Add the amounts on lines 20 through 22. Enter the total here. **Total miscellaneous** ▶ | **23** |

Summary of Itemized Deductions

(See Instructions on page 22.)

24 Add the amounts on lines 5, 10, 14, 18, 19, and 23. Enter your answer here. . . . | **24** |

25 If you checked Form 1040 { Filing Status box 2 or 5, enter $3,670 / Filing Status box 1 or 4, enter $2,480 / Filing Status box 3, enter $1,835 } | **25** |

26 Subtract line 25 from line 24. Enter your answer here and on Form 1040, line 34a. (If line 25 is more than line 24, see the Instructions for line 26 on page 22.) . . . ▶ | **26** |

For Paperwork Reduction Act Notice, see Form 1040 Instructions.   Schedule A (Form 1040) 1986

Annotations:

REPEALED, OR SUBJECT TO THE PASSIVE LOSS RULE, OR SUBJECT TO THE INVESTMENT INTEREST RULE. (CHAPTER THREE)

ALL OF THESE GO INTO THE 2% POT. (CHAPTER THREE)

SUCH AS EMPLOYEE BUSINESS EXPENSES AND TRAVEL EXPENSES. (CHAPTERS FIVE AND SIX)

A NEW SECTION FOR MOVING EXPENSES. (CHAPTER THREE)

THESE FIGURES ARE GOING UP. (CHAPTER THREE)

INDEX